GROUNDED

Published by Mortimer Books
An imprint of the Welbeck Publishing Group Limited
20 Mortimer Street
London W1T 3JW

ISBN 978-1-78739-586-2

Commissioning Editor: Victoria Marshallsay
Designer: Georgina Hewitt
Proofreader: Sarah Uttridge
Indexer: Angie Hipkin

A CIP catalogue for this book is available from the British Library.

Printed in China

10 9 8 7 6 5 4 3

GROUNDED

HOW CONNECTION WITH NATURE CAN IMPROVE OUR MENTAL AND PHYSICAL WELLBEING

RUTH ALLEN

MORTIMER

CONTENTS

INTRODUCTION

MY NATURE STORY

An emotional connection with nature matters. Not everyone can access therapy, but we can all benefit from access to the natural world. This is not a book about doing therapy outside, but how you can work with nature therapeutically, relationally. Wellbeing is experienced from the inside out and nature can provide us with a means of connecting with our inner landscape, re-energizing us when so much has become rational, formulated and sterilized. But first, I'd like to tell you about my own nature story.

As a child, I spoke to animals, read about animals and wrote stories about animals. The veil between our worlds was thin and papery, sometimes not there at all. I knew that not everyone spoke to animals, and that a day would come when I would have to grow up and forget my childish ways – but while it lasted I was self-contained, enchanted and content. As a teenager, my love of nature found a new awareness: fighting the oppression of animals took centre stage and I became interested in activism and advocacy. By adulthood, I was no longer talking to animals at all; instead, my attention switched to landscape, landforms and the dramatic, sometimes violent, processes of life on earth. By early adulthood, I had completed a degree in geology and was studying for a PhD on the erosion of the Himalayan mountains. Rather than talking to or immersing myself in nature, I chipped samples from natural forms and put them under a microscope. I separated particles and measured their chemical signatures. I was following a path that I hoped would take me to the wildest places in the world, but seemed to be taking me indoors to laboratories, where I was becoming cross-eyed, separated from nature, lost.

LOSING GROUND

Along the way, I was making poor decisions in my personal life, had suddenly lost my dad, and had almost given up believing that I would ever regain my wonder at the world. The beautiful world that had so captivated me as a child, that I believed in so passionately as a teenager, and that had enchanted me into a long but ultimately hollowing quest for scientific knowledge in early adulthood. My sense of purpose was gone and my relationship with nature all but shattered. I had lost the ground beneath my feet. I struggled to find a sense of direction and purpose in the world. I didn't know what I wanted anymore and lurched between hobbies and projects in a bid to find what I needed. I had spent years building a career that I could do, but not one that I loved or now enjoyed. There was a widening gap between who and where I was, and who and where I wanted to be; I dreamed about and was haunted by my unlived lives. I was grieving, guilty and disconnected.

FINDING LIGHT

I managed to rediscover the light through conscious, considered reconnection. It became essential for me to go back outside and to be in nature again in order to reconnect with the innate love that had been buried by the pressures of life. I needed to return to the basics, to remember what I loved and why, in the hope that in doing so I would find who or what I was trying to be: the person that was strong and capable, robust and focused, but also gentle and kind. The unshakeable me. The me who was safe with myself. So, I took my sadness, my losses, my loneliness and disconnection outside. I took it up hill after hill, into valleys, woodlands, and out to sea. I walked it around endlessly, at first slowly and then quickly, until that wasn't enough, and then I cycled it up and over passes. I lugged it up fells, over cols, down alpine switchbacks. I slept with it in tents, under the stars, and awoke with it in snowy wonderlands. I even herded alpacas with it for a year. All the while, I worked, focusing on the joy of nature I was starting to rediscover, and held tight to all the threads of possibility. I was *back in movement*. I stopped carrying all my emotion as baggage and started talking to it. I conversed with my sorrow as if it was another person. 'What do you want from me?' I would ask it. Of my guilt, 'When will you let me go?' Of my loneliness, 'What do you need?'

I needed to feel well in my body. I needed to feel in better control of my emotions and able to feel more joy than sadness. I needed to feel less fearful. I needed to understand my place in the world. I needed purpose. I needed meaning. I needed to like my life. I needed to feel present in the life I was living, rather than hankering after the one I wasn't. I needed to feel grounded – like I did when I was outside in nature, connecting with the things that had always made me feel good, and worthy, and like I belonged. I just needed *this*. *A lot more of this.* What I needed was already happening.

REDISCOVERING LOVE

By taking the big questions outside, I made space to hear the answers, and the answers gave my search some focus. I became more solid. I dealt better with stress. I was calmer. I was in better control of my emotions. I didn't hate myself anymore or keep punishing myself over wrong moves. I had my own back. I loved life again and I loved the journey I was being led along. Love was essential to my restoration – something our species does so well. Love made me want to talk to the world again, but not just to animals: I wanted to talk to people who were suffering. I wanted to help them make sense of their lives; I wanted to be alongside them. And this time, I wanted to do it *with nature*. No more labs. No more open-plan offices. No more committee meetings. I wanted to work with people, for people, with nature, for nature. In the years that followed, I refocused, retrained and relocated. I took big risks, gave up some big commitments in order to make space, and set about living an intentional, purposeful, contented life centred on compassion and a connection with nature. Reconnecting with nature wasn't a cure, it was a way back to conducting a decent relationship with myself and with others. My ability to translate that connection with nature into a meaningful way of being in the world was revitalizing.

HEALING THROUGH EXPERIENCE

I now adventure when I can, as this is my favourite way to stay grounded, but adventure is not the only way to connect with nature. I am interested in the phenomenology of experiencing nature: how you experience, what you experience, in the moment. But also why your experience is important or meaningful. This fascination with individual consciousness runs through my therapeutic practice. I am less interested in universal scientific truths or organizing principles than in the deeply personal experience of what it means to be alive in the world. I am also interested in what we love, and why: what speaks to us; what motivates us;

what heals us; what do we turn towards? In working with people therapeutically outdoors, I get a privileged insight into all of this – into how people experience life and nature, and indeed love, connection, and relationships. I am concerned less with how thoughts, feelings and emotions are stored or generated in the brain (although that's fun to explore, and can be helpful), and more with how they affect our mind, body and spirit. How you feel your way through the natural world can play a vital role in enhancing wellbeing and your sense of being grounded. To facilitate healing, I want to speak with your heart.

WHAT IS NATURE?

Nature is everything you are. Everything inside and outside. It is in and around you on every level, from your personal microbiome to the edges of the universe. It is the breath sending oxygen to your lungs and, over there, somewhere, a leopard licking its paw. It is tectonic plates moving, a planet dying, a fish nudging a pebble.

Nature is coming and going, and yet is irreducible. It just *is*. You are part of it whether you consider yourself 'interested in nature' or not (and my contention is that you are interested even if you don't know it), because if you have any interest in staying alive and living the life that is yours, through whatever means you have available to you, then you are interested in nature.

Nature resists compartmentalizing; while pecking orders exist, they are not the hierarchies of value or prestige that our species seeks to apply. Nature is as much the worm in your composter as it is the wilderness of your imagination. Nature is non-judgemental and non-discriminating. It is neither benevolent nor malevolent. It is sentient, conscious and feeling, and also none of those

things. Somehow it has *mind,* but it won't always communicate in language we understand. Nature is *happening* in every moment: not for you, but in you and alongside you, and also without you.

Nature is diverse across every conceivable marker and definition of diversity. Not one bit of it looks the same as you, though there may be similarities. It behaves without a consciousness of what behaviour is. Some people will tell you that nature is comforting, nourishing, providing, dependable. Others will tell you it is terrifying, punishing, hostile, withholding. A third group may have no sense of nature whatsoever, so profound is their disconnection. No position is factually correct or incorrect, each reflects the lived experience of its beholders.

FORGING A RELATIONSHIP

In this book, I am not aiming to tell you that nature is one thing or another, or what you should think about it. My hope is that you will feel what you feel and

craft your own relationship with nature, perhaps for the first time. What nature means to you will be unique based on your experience of being alive in the world. If nature has been kind to you, then you are likely to feel favourably towards it. If you have suffered in nature, then you might have a different perspective. If you haven't been shown anything of nature, you might have the largest barrier to break down, but also the greatest opportunity ahead of you.

A relationship is not one thing and neither are we: our experiences with nature can be as diverse as we are. My own relationship with nature has been an exciting affair over the years, though thankfully one unmarked by serious difficulty or damage. I haven't lost my home to a natural disaster or

lost a loved one to the elements. I have been given access to wild lands, and not held back from my desire to be outside. My lens is therefore positively disposed towards nature; a position of privilege. Many people in the world live in a natural context so diminished, polluted or controlled that their experiences will have been very different: I am mindful that not everyone has equal access, and that those of us who have are invited into the work of broadening this injustice.

That said, despite what you might have been led to believe, nature *does not belong to anyone*. It is borderless despite the lines we have drawn. It belongs to itself, just as you belong to yourself. At the same time, it is in us and we are our own access point; our only true way in is through a meaningful, respectful and reciprocal relationship. We can become grounded – calm, balanced, able to survive the trials of life – through an ongoing relationship with nature, ourselves and each other. Being grounded is good for us, and it is good for nature. Our planet, struggling to live under the conditions we have created, desperately needs us to reconnect and take steps towards repair.

USING OLD WISDOM

This book is a personal and professional testimony to what I know about becoming grounded and finding myself in nature. The themes I explore are included because they have been persistent within my life and my professional practice. This does not mean that they are an exhaustive list. A different type of person, in a different place, at a different time – even myself in future years – might make various additions or subtractions, or might place a greater emphasis on one theme over another. Also, the practical examples might change.

However, it is my hope that the themes I have included are somewhat universal. You will notice that none of them are 'new' but have longevity. After all, we have been talking about solitude for as long as there have been communities, and we have been discussing mystery for as long as we've had consciousness. Connecting with nature is nothing new; we are simply at a point of remembering after a long sleep. My intention is to bring fresh eyes to old wisdom, and to bring the lessons, joy and solace of nature to a new audience.

HOW TO USE THIS BOOK

In this book, as in therapy, I don't have all the answers. In fact, I'm confident enough to say I don't have any for definite: just suggestions, tools, approaches and inklings – the wisdom borne of a little bit of experience working on myself and with others. The answers are for you to find with my support; I can't do it for you, as you well know.

What follows is not the secret formula to *becoming grounded* but a collection of waymarkers. You can choose to follow their guidance into different terrains; each will take you down its own path for a while. You can pursue the things you are drawn to and turn away from those you are not. How you piece the journey together is up to you, and no doubt you will find other markers and detours along the way. You will make your own formula to develop the qualities of being grounded that interest you. You will modify: that's okay. Becoming grounded is a uniquely personal exercise within the context of your own life. Just as *grounded* is no one thing, there is also no one way to get there.

There will be things to consider and do, and the level of your engagement is up to you. There is no time limit and no rush: you have a lifetime. This is not meant to be hard labour. Change will come less from trying and more from your growing awareness of what it means to be grounded – more yourself – by putting ideas into practice, little by little every day. As with all worthwhile things, nature teaches us that changes come in their own time, as you begin to experience yourself differently, as you interrupt your routines and habits, and as you experiment with new ways of being.

In therapy, I have a mantra: meet people where they're at, not where they want to be, or where they were in the past. Improving your connection with nature, finding yourself and becoming grounded is possible whoever you are, wherever you are, and from wherever you have been, or are going to. You don't have to be wealthy, athletic, 'outdoorsy', from an adventurous family or of any particular age demographic, gender, ethnicity, nationality or sexuality: the words over the following pages are for all of us. Be honest with yourself about your starting point and proceed from there. If you have no connection with nature, then now is the time to begin; if you have a deep connection, great, your job is to take it deeper still. When it comes to being grounded, no one is ahead or behind; we start where we are.

PRESENCE

WHAT ARE WE LOOKING FOR?

The basis of good therapy – conducted inside or outside – is being present and paying attention, that is, really listening to what the other person has to tell you. Sometimes this is communicated through words, and other times not. Sometimes it is relayed via embodied language – the energetic sense of things, the words that are left unsaid. It begins with the first email, or the moment you shake hands, and continues throughout the work as you get to know each other.

Increasingly, I have noticed clients saying in clear words, through gestures, expressions, or conversely by articulating all the things they are not, that they want to feel *grounded*. In my experience, very few people are looking for cures for loss, change, suffering or death – there is an understanding that these are the existential givens of life. Instead, most people are looking to alleviate the symptoms of these realities – for a way to *live with* the fact of loss and the presence of pain and to become calm, balanced and centred within the experience of their lives. In short, they are looking to weather the storm: to cope. People who are stressed; people who are anxious; people who are depressed; people who are confused. People who are fraught, forgetful or floundering. People who find themselves emotionally on the edge, and nowhere near the calm centre of themselves. They are all asking in many different ways: 'How can I live with life?'

Occasionally they might say, 'You seem very grounded. How do you do it?' With time, I have come to understand that only a few are asking for the basic instructions for grounding (though this is a start, and where we begin). What they are really asking for is the secret to becoming more present, resilient, calm, balanced (and many more things besides) within the broad context of their whole lives. They are looking for a solution to the problems of stress, anxiety, worry, busyness, responsibility, loss, loneliness, disconnection, pain, or constant change. They are looking for purpose, meaning and direction. They are looking to hold on to a sense of themselves when everything else is awry. They are looking for the best part of themselves. They are looking to feel safe and secure enough to commune joyfully with what *is*. They are looking for what we are all looking for.

BEING 'GROUNDED'

'The world cannot be discovered by a journey of miles, no matter how long, but only by a spiritual journey, a journey of one inch, very arduous and humbling and joyful, by which we arrive at the ground at our feet, and learn to be at home.' Wendell Berry

Putting your feet on the ground. Sitting or standing up straight with a sense that your weight is pushing downwards into the earth. Perhaps moving one foot in front of the other in a slow walk. These are the simplest ways of making contact with both yourself and the rest of nature – of grounding. *Making contact* is the most direct way to be connected – to be in *a relationship* – with yourself and the living planet. Grounding is a physical act, a technique, a method, a practice in pursuit of a particular destination. To be grounded is to have arrived at a solid place in the present. To be grounded is to come home – to yourself; to nature.

Being grounded is a concept that encompasses a nebulous range of qualities that we might attribute to a person who is approaching, living and experiencing their life in a particular way. It is something you can be in the moment, but also something you can practise your whole life. It is a difficult concept to describe in theory, being more easily recognized in person – either by its absence (see the story of my early adult years in the introduction) or by bringing to mind someone you know who embodies grounded qualities.

To be grounded is a way of being – a *gestalt* – that encompasses our emotional states and responses, our relationships with others, our beliefs about the world and ourselves, and our approach to living. It is no doubt more besides. You can understand 'being grounded' as a facet of our general wellbeing. Just as being grounded describes the holistic solidity of a person and their life, the concept of wellbeing seeks to describe an overall sense of physical, psychological and social wellness that goes beyond the simple absence of illness or disease. In 2008, the New Economics Foundation highlighted five key actions linked to wellbeing that also correlate with the pursuit of becoming grounded: *connect; be active; take notice; keep learning*; and *give*. You will notice in this book that grounding through nature also touches on these areas of wellbeing. By connecting with nature, we become more connected to ourselves.

Becoming grounded is about taking a broad look at the whole landscape of our lives, as well as focusing on the specific terrain. It is about going beyond purely intellectual insight and making discoveries that are felt in every part of our bodies. It is recognizing that the feeling of being grounded comes from attending to all of the ways we are left ungrounded by the life we are living.

This need not be as daunting as it sounds. Becoming grounded is less about perfection in a few specific areas than achieving 'enough' in a variety. Being grounded is less about specific accomplishments, and more about how you *are* in any given situation. Being grounded is everything that you are, whatever happens.

To be grounded is to return time and time again to the present, because the present, and our ability to stay within in it, continually shifts. Most of us find it incredibly hard to stay psychologically in the present with deep awareness for any length of time without defaulting to worrying or wishing. By its nature, the present is fleeting, ephemeral, shape-shifting; paired with minds and bodies that are also restless, prone to agitation and distraction, it is no wonder that being grounded is a state that develops over time though the continual practice of *coming back*. You will undoubtedly wander away: there may be hours, days, weeks or even years of disconnection and feeling ungrounded. I know this. It is not a reason to be hard on yourself and compound your suffering. The invitation is simply to come back; time and again. To reconnect with what is in front of you to be experienced, felt and lived. Nature shows us how to do this and offers us a place to *be* and *become*.

The following activities will help you consider the qualities of groundedness that you might want to explore yourself, as well as the barriers to feeling grounded. This where your project begins and will leave you with a better sense of the landscape around and ahead of you.

> **Becoming grounded is about taking a broad look at the whole landscape of our lives, as well as focusing on the specific terrain.**

WHAT DOES A 'GROUNDED' PERSON LOOK LIKE?

- Has healthy mastery over their emotions.
- Can manage themselves in relationships with others.
- Not easily influenced; unlikely to conform.
- Carries life's mishaps and quandaries lightly.
- Operates with a sense of perspective.
- Demonstrates resilience and robustness.
- Possesses a sense of safety in the world.
- Maintains balance and stability in many aspects of life.
- Active rather than reactive.
- Has a high tolerance for stress or is seemingly less affected by stress.
- Reliable and trustworthy.
- Relatively unshakeable and calm in a crisis.
- Content in their own skin.
- Communicates a healthy sense of self-worth.
- Able to tolerate and work with their weaknesses and perceived failures.
- Appears to embody a sense of peace; others feel calm around them.
- Often humble and willing to hand attention to others.
- Respects themselves and others in words and actions.
- Encouraging and supportive of others.
- Boundaried but not inflexible and closed.
- Rooted but open to possibility and debate.
- Has a sense of what's 'right' – an inner moral compass.
- Lives and works with a sense of purpose and direction.

HOW GROUNDED ARE YOU?

1. Looking at the 'grounded' list on page 28, how many of these qualities do you recognize in yourself? Be generous, no one is grounded all of the time. Are there any other grounded attributes that you could add to your own list?

2. Make a note of the qualities you would like to develop as single, simple words. You might like to journal thoughts that arise as you consider the qualities that appeal to you. Time spent reflecting upon the words you have noted will give you some direction for the type of thoughts and behaviours you might need to develop to express these qualities more fully in your life.

3. There are things that can make us feel ungrounded too. Make a list of five things in your life that leave you feeling ungrounded. Be specific. It might be a relationship, the job you're doing, the events that are unfolding around you, experiences you have had in the past.

BEGIN WITH THE SIMPLE ACT OF GROUNDING

This book is an exploration of how a connection with nature can foster the long-term practice of being grounded. My approach advocates going outside more and bringing what you've experienced inward. But there are many ways to ground yourself. Enjoying the company of good friends can be grounding; so too, regular journaling, having a quiet cup of coffee, time in the gym, cooking a meal, or using essential oils, to name just a few routes. You do not have to be outside to do something that grounds you, and neither is connection with nature the only way.

A grounding activity in the truest sense is one that invites you to notice what is happening inside you, and around you, and that brings you into contact with the present through your senses and your breath. It makes use of your human nature; so, taking nature out of a conversation about grounding is impossible. To be grounded is, by simplest definition, to be in contact with the ground, which is a basic way of being connected or in a *relationship*. Gravity keeps us here and does half the work. Contact is already made; all you have to do is add more awareness.

The link between body and earth provides a practical, foundational basis on which to start our training. It encourages us to arrive in the present moment; everything else builds upon it.

Throughout your time with this book you can use or adapt this simple technique as often as is useful in your journey to becoming grounded. When you feel yourself becoming ungrounded, feel your stress or anxiety levels rising, or simply wish to mark the start of a day outside, then this simple exercise is perfect for the job. Grounding yourself is a healthy and subversive act of disruption in a busy world that will always be conspiring to distract and unground you.

ARRIVE AT THE GROUND

I like to do this simple activity barefoot on compacted ground or grass. You may prefer sand, mud or shallow water. You may prefer to keep your shoes on, or to sit down instead of stand. You may wish to use your hands instead of your feet. Your choices might be dictated by mood. Be playful.

GROUNDING EXERCISE

Start by reading this activity through once or twice to familiarize yourself, and then begin:

1. Standing with your feet hip-width apart to create a solid stance, take a few moments to 'arrive' in the physical space. Close your eyes if this feels appropriate and safe; invite your breath to become deeper and slower.

2. As you breathe to a depth that feels comforting and soothing, turn your attention inwards away from the noise around you and notice any sensations within your body without judgement. Breathe into those places if you can and breathe out.

3. Ensure your feet are in as much contact with the ground as they can be. Spread your toes so that you can feel the ground across all of the soles of your feet. Notice the sensations in your feet and lower legs; see if you can send these downwards with your breath.

4. Now spend some time inviting a feeling of solidity and strength into your body and sending that energy downwards as you breathe in and out, pulling the in-breath up through your feet to the top of your head, and then sending it back down again. Envision this as a beam of light running down from the air above you, through your body and deep into the earth as roots.

5. Bring your attention to the contact your feet are making with the earth and see if you can imagine and feel the weight of the earth coming up to *meet* your feet. Understand that this is *contact*.

6. Take as long as you wish to feel relaxed in this activity, enjoying your free-flowing breath and the feel of your body on the ground. Visualize yourself as a tree grounded in the earth or a favourite plant in the soil.

This is a simple way of connecting physically, energetically, psychologically, and perhaps even emotionally and spiritually, with the planet you are living on. The practice can be as quick or as slow as you wish. There is no rush.

CONNECTION

LOST CONNECTIONS

Living in the twenty-first century, our lost connections are plentiful and diverse: we have lost our connection to the land and to nature; we have lost our sense of place in the natural world, and also our understanding of how we fit into the ecological web. This is symptomatic of losing our connection with ourselves and with each other.

We have lost connection with our communities and our sense of belonging to each other. We have lost connection with our intuition and inner wildness, with our bodies, and how we link our minds and bodies. We have lost connection with our true feelings, with who we really are and what we really want, believe and find meaningful. We have lost connection with the wisdom of how to heal, and how to live fulfilling and meaningful lives. Modern, highly urbanized, indoor-based, consumer-orientated, socially atomized, goal-orientated, productivity driven, geographically fractured, digitally mediated living has disconnected us. While none of it has been intentional, the result is the same. In moving indoors and being kept busy, we have forgotten about nature and what it means to be active and present in the natural world. We have looked away, and our disconnection from the intrinsic qualities of nature has made us unhappy and unwell.

COMING BACK

The good news is that we are, at individual and community levels at least, becoming engaged in the long-term process of *coming back*. People are beginning to get outside more often and are rediscovering their love of nature. We are finding new and creative ways to be outside – devising new sports, new adventures, new ways of connecting with nature's abundance. In some cases, we are even starting to use what has disconnected us to reconnect. What if we could incorporate technology into our relationship with the outside world without it taking us away from nature? What if phones could encourage us outside to locate new things to see and do, but then we leave them aside while we engage with wildness? What if we could formulize the benefits of nature in a way that suits our scientific paradigm, and encourages us into ways of living that go beyond the need to be productive? All these things are happening and more.

In doing so, we are realizing the many ways we have forgotten the preciousness of nature that we are destroying. We are seeing what happens when we view ourselves as separate and intrinsically apart from nature: we forget to value and protect it. We treat nature as an object of consumption, or as a staging ground for our ambition, rather than a community of equal *subjects*. We forget this *'I-Thou'* relationship that characterizes healthy connection.

In this age of disconnection, the natural world can help us reconnect with so much that risks being lost, including good relationships with ourselves and with others, which in turn can ground us and deliver a rooted sense of wellbeing. A nature-connected human species starts with the action of individuals deciding to do things differently: it's never too late to decide to do things differently.

HOW IS NATURE GOOD FOR US?

That contact with nature is good for us should be obvious. We exist in a vast, complex and interconnected natural web. As a species we come from wild lands, and over time have moved into diverse environments across the planet; as a result, many of us instinctively know that nature is part of us somewhere and that time in nature helps us feel well.

Nature is good for our physical, emotional, psychological, social and spiritual wellbeing, and this has been confirmed in study after peer-reviewed study looking at natural settings that include open countryside, wilderness spaces, gardens and allotments, parks, blue spaces such as sea and rivers, and urban green spaces.

The most cited benefits of time spent in nature, or of taking in natural views, include promoting a positive mood, a reduction in stress and anxiety, increased self-esteem, improved personal resilience, and better social functioning and inclusion. Studies have also revealed that nature-based wellbeing interventions have multiple outcomes: that is, what is good for your physical health is good for your mental and emotional health, and vice versa.

You might say that immersion in nature offers you good value for time

'We are not strengthened by our connection to nature, but weakened by our separation from it'.

and money, as it provides a range of holistic benefits rather than just the one you might have been aiming for at the outset. This is what biologist Clemens G. Arvay calls the 'healing code of nature'. He states: 'We are not strengthened by our connection to nature, but weakened by our separation from it'. This is more important that we might realize. Nature should not be seen as a beneficial added extra that we have gathered evidence for, but as a vital component of holistic health that we have moved away from, to our detriment.

Here are a few ways in which nature has been shown, scientifically, to be beneficial for human health and wellbeing. New research is published all the time. I have separated the benefits into psychological and physiological, but as you will see, they are interrelated.

PSYCHOLOGICAL BENEFITS OF TIME SPENT IN NATURE

- Reduces stress and promotes feelings of calm, healing and regeneration through activation of the 'rest and digest' parasympathetic nervous system.
- Increases general feelings of health and happiness, including eudaimonic wellbeing – giving value to life.
- Reduces symptoms of depression and anxiety by increasing Vitamin D levels through exposure to sunlight, by providing contact with the microbial properties of soil and by allowing interaction with animals.
- Improves mood and promotes positive emotions through experiences such as contact with animals or observing beauty.
- Promotes the production of neurotransmitters such as dopamine, of endorphins, and of the bonding hormone oxytocin.
- Allows for the development of skills and coping strategies, needed as we navigate our life environments.
- Improves and restores normal levels of attention; reduces distractibility.
- Increases social connectivity, reducing social isolation and loneliness.

PHYSIOLOGICAL BENEFITS OF TIME SPENT IN NATURE

- Aerobic activities, such as walking or running, lower blood pressure and blood sugar levels.
- Decreases prevalence of lifestyle diseases such as heart disease, diabetes and hypertension.
- Stimulates the production of hormones associated with a reduction in coronary heart disease and Alzheimer's.
- Boosts the immune system by increasing the production of helpful natural killer cells and anticancer proteins.
- Hospitals with green views can reduce the need for painkillers.
- The generation of awe can reduce inflammation in the body.
- Contact with animals can improve heart-attack and critical-illness recovery in healthcare settings.

THE BENEFITS OF NATURAL VIEWS

The Green Exercise Research Team at the University of Essex (UK) have highlighted three types of beneficial engagement with nature: natural views, contact with nearby nature, and participation in nature-based activities. Natural vistas, which can be particularly useful in hospitals or care settings, have been shown to help us recover from fatigue, enhance cognition, reduce stress levels and generate an overall improvement in mental wellbeing.

This very much justifies the time I love to spend staring out of windows that overlook hills and trees. More interesting still is that simply looking at *pictures* of nature has been shown to improve mood and self-esteem. Pictures that feature water are thought to be especially helpful. The physiological benefits include reducing heart rate and blood pressure and having a relaxing effect on the cardiovascular system and autonomic function.

Next time you're near an art gallery, why not pop in and seek out a nature painting for a quick pick-me-up. Alternatively, spend some time savouring photos taken from a previous nature trip, or seek out beautiful natural photos on social media that make you feel good about yourself and the world.

THE TOPOPHILIA THEORY

Related to biophilia, topophilia was a word first offered by W. H. Auden to describe our innate bond with *place*. As with biophilia, the exact evolutionary processes at work are still being researched, but topophilia may explain the useful benefits of becoming bonded with our local area and local nature through place-based living – through enduring presence and attention. In this way, we come to know how our local place functions in terms of its natural and cultural life, and thus grow familiar and more dependent on its abundance and benefits for us as its human inhabitants.

To develop a topophilic bond to place is not a short-term project, but it could begin today. Why not spend more time getting to know the nature in your local area. What is nearby, what happens as the seasons turn, what does your place offer you, how do you feel when you are in it? Living more locally in our place and understanding its benefits may be a vital part of the solution to lowering our carbon footprint and re-establishing local biodiversity.

THE BIOPHILIA THEORY

In recent years, the benefits of nature for our wellbeing have become clear, but our connection to nature runs even deeper than science can prove at present. The theory of biophilia described by psychologist Erich Fromm, and elaborated by biologist E.O. Wilson, suggests that we have a genetically determined affinity with the natural world, and that we all possess an innate tendency to seek connection with what is vital beyond the human species. Biophilia proposes that it is our natural love of life and nature that sustains life itself, as we seek to nurture and love all that is alive. It also explains our biophobic responses – our natural repulsion to things that might harm us.

That we are instinctively drawn to life, even though it is messy and complex, feels obvious to me; but as we have begun to pursue indoor lives, and allowed technology to dominate, the energy devoted to supporting our biophilic tendencies has decreased. This has fuelled our disconnection from nature, reduced our physical and emotional wellness, diminished our ability to find meaning in nature, and caused the current ecological crisis. We have become estranged from our own innate, protective love of the world. I believe that many of us feel a deep sadness about this loss – we feel an eco-grief , a sense of *species loneliness*. Some of us are already in touch with that sadness, others may experience the sensation of it, but not know that this is what they are grieving for.

It stands to reason that when our home is sick, we are also sick. If we are to make both well again, we must reconnect with our biophilic tendency. To thrive, we need to get back in touch with our innate, irreducible, 'hard-wired' longing for the world. The health of humanity and our planet requires us to feel the tug of aliveness *out there* that echoes through our DNA, and to stop resisting its pull.

NATURE IS AN EQUAL PARTNER

Clients often come into therapy asking for tools and techniques to help them think positively, feel better, or maintain healthier behaviours. They are looking for something to get them from where they are to where they want to be, recognizing that what is missing has a 'thingness' to it. It's not as simple as just 'think differently' or 'change the way you feel'. Instinct tells them it's something with substance, a set of actions, an instrument, a thing to *do*, that will get them to where they want to be.

I understand this, and sometimes it's possible to devise a five-step plan to unpick a unhealthy habit. However, when the solution is to become more grounded – to become more solid, contented, calm and all the other things we associate with being grounded – the tool and technique I advocate is to develop a connection with nature. In fact, more than this – it is to cultivate a *relationship* with nature. Within this there will be actions and things to do, but they will be in service to the *relationship* you are building with nature in order to discover the best of yourself within it.

The problem with thinking about nature in terms of tools and techniques is that the natural world is not simply a resource for our use. In imagining that the planet is here to serve us, provide for us, and accommodate all our desires, we have enslaved it and stripped it down for parts. We are often guilty of not looking after our tools – sometimes we clean them and put them away carefully, other times we just throw them back in the cupboard, leave them to go rusty, or fail to service them until they break, at which point we curse them and buy a new one.

> **Having a connection with nature is a way to get you from where you are to where you want to be.**

The limitation of seeing nature as a tool for our healing and self-discovery is that we can fall into the trap of thinking of it as a replaceable resource. A greater offense is to have imagined it was ever our tool to *use* in the first place.

With this in mind, I invite you to use the term 'tool' lightly, and not to stretch the metaphor beyond its function. My intention is for it to help you understand that having a connection with nature is a way to get you from where you are to where you want to be. The real aim is to go beyond notions of utility and to develop a language of *relationship*.

As a therapist, I see repeatedly that relationships are central to healing. It is what happens within a relationship – what the two people involved make of it and do with it – that effects change. Connection is the missing link.

While relationships are created between people, we also carry them within us as sources of kindness, love and wisdom. If we can let love move inside us, it can drive us towards the betterment of ourselves and of others, creating a cycle of compassion and reciprocal connection. This is how I hope you will see the benefit of nature in your life – a grounding, virtuous circle.

DEEPENING OUR RELATIONSHIP WITH NATURE

While simply being in a natural environment is beneficial to human health, it is a deeper contact and engagement – connection – with nature that has been shown to promote long-term improvements in mental health and emotional wellbeing.

The most up-to-date research from the University of Derby, UK, shows that simply going outside is not enough to improve mental health on its own, it's what you *do* with the time outdoors that matters. Nature *engagement* is how we access the goodness of nature for mental wellbeing – we need to develop a meaningful, more emotional, relationship. Time is needed, true moments of connection matter. The same researchers also found that connection with nature might be *predictive* of an absence of depression and anxiety.

The research isolated five predictors for increased connection with nature and the benefits that this brings: engagement of the senses, exposure to beauty, assignation of meaning, and evocation of emotion and of compassion. While this book has been developed independently of the University of Derby study, the themes explored reflect the pathways above. I am particularly interested in stimulating the pathways of emotion and of meaning – helping clients understand what being in nature can do, or could mean, and what emotions it can generate or release.

CULTIVATING A RELATIONSHIP OF WORTH

No relationship of worth is sustained by first contact alone. No depth is created through dipping in and out mindlessly with no care. No benefit is felt without an investment in time, love, openness, curiosity and patience. When we connect with nature, others or ourselves, a spark is ignited, emotions get involved, and

we set off on a journey of what it is to know and be known. Connection with nature helps us feel closer to wildness – to the intrinsic freedom of nature. Like a good human to human relationship, a relationship with nature offers each one of us the chance to become grounded, to heal and to flourish.

I see 'grounded' as a byword for what it means to be in a *good relationship* with the earth, and by extension with ourselves and with others.

The importance of the positive emotions generated by conducting a good relationship – in this case with nature – should not to be underestimated, as these influence the function of our bodies, our nervous system and our brains. We need to be able to regulate our emotions to help us respond to life as it unfolds, healthily and appropriately. Nature is particularly effective in aiding emotional regulation, especially in soothing the sympathetic nervous system (which controls stress and anxiety) and activating the parasympathetic nervous system (which controls our 'rest and digest' function). This mirrors the benefits of the best human relationships: we offer each other help and support during times of stress, just like nature.

COMMUNITY GARDENING: SOCIAL AND NATURAL CONNECTION

Good social connections matter just as much as connecting with nature, particularly for reducing feelings of social isolation or loneliness. If you don't have a green space of your own, if you know deep down you would benefit from more social contact, or if you simply want to spend more time with others, consider finding a local community garden or contacting your local Wildlife Trust. Community green places are becoming increasingly popular and many urban areas have projects you can join. They are an amazing way to connect with other people, to get your hands in the earth, to nurture life and food, and to contribute to your local community and wildlife.

REWILDING: THE CALL TO CONNECTION

Rewilding our lives is a means of rekindling our inbuilt affinity with the natural world – our innate biophilic tendency. It involves the intention and action of exploring and embracing the wild within us in order to deepen our connection with nature, for the mutual benefit of ourselves and the rest of nature. The nature of which we are a part. It is not about going backwards, but about making space for nature, with a renewed sense of its importance, in the time ahead. We could also call this *wilding* our lives.

The urge to rewild can lead us back into connection with nature. A fundamental requirement of ecological rewilding is the provision of natural 'corridors' that link wild places, giving wildlife a route along which to move, seek food, thrive and spread. In our own lives, we also need corridors: psychological and emotional pathways that run from the outside in, and inside out. These corridors help us to access the benefits of nature, breaking down the belief that we are separate from the natural world, and that it exists separately from us. These pathways allow a throughflow of wildness that is recognizable and shared: wild becomes us.

To re-establish our connection with nature, we need to let ourselves become re-enchanted with the world like we were as children. We need to ask 'Why?' and

We need to see beauty in the smallest things; to see the miracle of life on a living planet hurtling through the universe.

'How?' but also to give our hearts and minds over to wonder and awe. We need to see beauty in the smallest things; to see the miracle of life on a living planet hurtling through the universe.

There was a time when nature was more wondrous, when we were deeply enchanted by the natural world, when our eyes lit up not because we knew the scientific explanation for something, but because it was just beautiful, or weird, or unlikely, or unexplained and magical. In the scientific paradigm of our age, enchantment has diminished in favour of a more clinical and verifiable knowledge base. Our desire to prove and achieve everything has pushed out playfulness. But playful curiosity generates enchantment, and both are a renewable source of desire for *more nature*.

Re-enchantment has perhaps also, objectively, become more difficult in recent times. Our accrued evidence base now tells us that the earth is suffering more significantly than ever before. We are facing catastrophic species loss and the collapse of biodiversity. Habitats are being destroyed at levels we can barely comprehend, despite the translation of 'football fields per second'. The climate is warming to unprecedented levels, the ice caps melting, the oceans heating, and at the same time filling with plastics and other pollutants. Signs of collapse are all around us. It is hard to find enchantment when looking at the world involves so much loss and sadness. How can this be enchanting? How can we be child-like now that we are adults with guilt, contrition, despair, anger? These are valid and important questions. Just as the nature of our connection has to fit the age in which we live, so too does our re-enchantment. We have to find a way to rewild our connection to nature, our minds, bodies, longings and purposes, despite the mess, and to repair the connection. The following chapters are, in their own ways, part of the rewilding story. We need to become both wild and grounded to deal with what lies ahead: nature is not gone yet.

NEARBY NATURE MATTERS

'Every touch of nature deeply stirs currents of feelings within us, in the same manner as a light breeze stirs the canopy of a tree, the rustle a subtle witness to the atmosphere's restlessness.' Andreas Weber

Researchers in the area of nature and human health all agree that local green space and 'nearby nature' – whether an urban park or a rural wilderness – are vital for wellbeing. While we tend to ascribe greater value to some aspects of nature over others (because humans, by instinct seem to like categories and hierarchies), in reality wild nature is valuable wherever it is found. What matters to you and your wellbeing is that you seek out what's local to you, and supplement it with what's further afield. The nature that is most beneficial to you is that which you can access and connect with, wherever you are. If you have a park, visit it. The best nature for our human health is that which we actually encounter.

Exposure to green space in urban areas – visiting local parks, walking through green areas has been shown to moderate the effects of socio-economic inequality, and perceived neighbourhood greenness is strongly associated with better physical and mental health. Local green spaces are good for promoting longevity, stress recovery, providing protection from future stress, lowering mental distress, and improving concentration. In areas with plenty of green space, people have been shown to secrete lower levels of the stress hormone cortisol and are three times more likely to be physically active outdoors. It pays to notice and give your time to nearby nature wherever you are: no amount of time and attention is too little.

TAKE A TINY GREEN BREAK

Consider adding a 'tiny green break'
into your existing routine. These green
buffers within urban living have been
shown to immediately reduce stress
and can be as simple as adding ten
minutes of green time into your daily
commute. Make the effort to visit a
park during your lunch break, find a
natural view to focus on, notice flowers,
plants and birds; feel the weather. If
you combine these actions with writing
down a few things in nature you are
grateful for at the same time, you will
be supercharging your connection with
nature and your feeling of wellbeing.

MOVEMENT

ENGAGING THE BODY

It is vital to engage our bodies in the pursuit of wellbeing, not just for physical health, but because our bodies regulate our emotions. It is through our bodies that we sense the world. If we want to become grounded, we have to involve them in the process. Thinking will only get us so far.

It may seem an obvious point, but when we walk into the counselling room or when we engage in therapy outside, we enter the space with our bodies. We enter *in* our bodies, but are often disconnected from them. The bodies we bring are moving, twitching, agitating, carrying all of our joys, pains, hopes and anxieties. Verbal dialogue is used in therapy to describe the lives we've lived and are living, but our bodies also have something vital to communicate – we can *talk* through them. It is our bodies that send messages to our brain about how to feel and behave. They are the primary generator, regulator and storehouse of our emotions.

Love, fear, anxiety, stress, worry, anger, grief, pain and trauma are all felt in the body and can be communicated through physical symptoms as well as words. What we believe about ourselves moves in our bodies, as does what we believe about others, what

we connect with and care about, what repels and revolts us, what we fear and what we long for. Everything that we are – our personality, our behaviour, our cognition, our emotion – and everything that has happened to us, lives in our bodies, in the container of ourselves. As the psychiatrist Bessel van der Kolk memorably noted: the body keeps the score.

Without being present and, as far as possible 'here' in our bodies, even with their aches and pains, it is difficult to be grounded. The importance of the body is why I try and take my clients outside. I want your body to be part of the process of becoming emotionally well, and that involves doing what our bodies also do well – moving. Physical movement sparks our feelings and brings us into deeper contact with ourselves and with others. It is through movement that we connect with the people and the world around us.

> What you know is also moving in you; it is alive in your body through sensation. This is 'body knowing'.

UNDERSTANDING MOVEMENT

I deeply believe that *movement is life, and life is a searching movement*. As I write those words, I can feel the truth of what I know innately about movement expand into my chest. My lungs fill, I take a deep breath. Something is rising in my throat, the tops of my arms and shoulders tingle. I feel a bit heady. A bit shivery. This is sensation: the thoughts I am having *about* movement are *in* movement through me as physical sensations. This is the same for other things I know, and it's the same for you too. What you know is also moving in you; it is alive in your body through sensation. This is 'body knowing'.

Our bodies can offer a window into our minds in a way that words can't. Typically, our brains are conditioned into certain ways of thinking: we take on the values, beliefs, opinions and judgements of others from the moment we learn language. Words generated by the mind are therefore not always an indicator of what we truly think or feel. Our bodies are simpler systems in many respects. While they are still complex and can go awry (as in the case of trauma), if we pay attention to our bodies as well as our minds we can get a more complete picture of ourselves. Supporting wellbeing through the body is just as important as treating the mind – they are not distinct but work together – and anyone who has ever felt anxious, or has ever felt love, will know that the body desperately wants to be heard.

BREATH AS THE FIRST MOVEMENT OF LIFE

Everything that is alive is in movement. Whether at the level of multiplying cells, or the level of taking a walk through the fields. When movement ends for the last time, in our organs and our synapses, we call this death. Movement is life. As humans we breathe in and we breathe out, and this is the fundamental movement of our being. Breathing makes all other processes and actions possible in our blood, heart and brain. If we had no movement in breath, there would be no things to do, no dreams to aim for, no people to love. Just as seeds germinate and trees respire, these are all ways of moving through life and of generating further movement, inside and out. The breath is an important element in many ancient traditions and systems of healing, and this simplest of movements is an intrinsic part of the grounding technique and many holistic health treatments. There are few things simpler and sweeter than a deep breath of fresh, natural air.

WE ARE FOREVER IN MOVEMENT

Every seed fights to live, and to do so it must move outwards; it must move *towards*. Towards the light, towards nutrients, towards maturity. It is also true that in moving forwards we are moving closer to death. This can be a heart-wrenching and worrying existential dilemma that we must all come to terms with in order to live our fullest lives. Nature can help us with the task by encouraging us to appreciate the inevitable, life's enduring cyclicity, and seasonality. The endless movement of nature can offer us some peace.

In the time that we are alive, you could say that our 'being' in the world has a direction. We may move on linear, circular, or messy paths – down dead ends and cul-de-sacs – but in a greater sense, we are always moving *towards*. Indeed, many people come to therapy because they have either stopped moving forwards (and are pained by it), or are moving towards something that feels out of control or unhealthy.

It takes the leverage of everything we know to move through our growth stages and to live life, and the things we don't know we have to learn. We are seeking from the moment that we open our eyes to the world. We are seeking friends, partners, jobs, homes. We are seeking community, connection and commitment. We are seeking meaning, purpose, vocation. We are seeking ways to avoid dying prematurely. We are seeking our dreams, our healing, our sense of being somebody in the world to others and for ourselves. We are seeking to fill the gaps and empty hole inside ourselves. We are seeking a sense of being 'enough', of validation, and of evidence that it's going to be okay. We are searching for external things that will make us feel better on the inside, and internal things that will help the outside feel bearable. This is why I say life is a *searching movement*.

The fact that we are forever in movement makes it even more important that we learn to come to ground. So that as well as being in movement we have a way to slow down, to connect to the present, to be enough as we are, and to rest in being.

BE MORE BEE

A simple, effective and nature-inspired breath exercise I love for alleviating stress and anxiety is inspired by the humble Indian black bee. Anxiety and stress can shorten our breath and cause chest-tightness, but this simple, breath-lengthening exercise taken from the yogic tradition, where it is known as *Bhramari pranayama*, can induce instant relaxation and help us feel grounded. As well as alleviating stress, this breathing exercise – which can be performed at any time for any duration – is believed to effectively treat anger and hypertension, reduce blood pressure and calm the nerves. It also stimulates the all-important vagus nerve. It is great for achieving clarity and confidence, and finding your voice.

1. Sit comfortably with a straight back and a relaxed face or a gentle smile.
2. Place your index fingers on the cartilage between your ears and cheeks.
3. Take a deep breath inward to a depth that feels comfortable, and as you exhale press the cartilage and make a humming 'M' sound like a bee.
4. Repeat as desired; at the end sit quietly and notice any changes in your mood.

As you do this exercise you should notice the soothing vibrations in your nose, face and elsewhere in your body. This is a great exercise to practise when you are alone, so that you can really connect with the sensations in your body, as well as the sound.

LEARNING FROM THE BODY OF NATURE

To talk about the body is to speak politically, and so we must try and speak clearly, wisely and generously. Bodies have been objectified, enslaved and abused throughout history, and so when I invite you to think about the body, to feel your body, or to recognize your own physical and emotional movement as it lives and breathes in your body, then I do so knowing that this isn't easy. We have become disconnected from our bodies, and sometimes this has been a protective, survival mechanism.

STARTING ANEW WITH SELF-COMPASSION

To come to a new conversation around body and movement with compassion and care, I find it helpful to first spend some time considering the body of nature. It is infinitely diverse: nimbly jointed insects; nervous, quick-footed squirrels; slender stalks of grass; the massive form of mountains; the unexpected grace of blue whales; the tall and upright presence of a pine tree. The body of nature is more heterogeneous than we can imagine when we focus only on ourselves. Nature has no word for misshapen or flawed. Beyond our species, the body of nature is so varied across so many millions of species and individuals that any notion of 'normal' becomes untenable and nonsensical.

Movement within nature is equally varied. We are relatively rare in our bipedalism, with most terrestrial animals moving on four legs, and a great many others swimming, crawling, bouncing, or flying. Some species cover very little ground but are nevertheless constantly in movement; others have very few parts to move at all. As humans, we are quick to make judgements and to categorize things into good/bad, better/worse, worthy/unworthy. We do this in regard to our bodies and we do it in relation to what movement we consider 'best'.

> **Nature is profoundly non-judgemental. It doesn't care how you look, what you wear, what speed you move at, the colour of your skin, the size of your body, it's capability.**

We become territorial about who has the best practice, whose class is the best, or which sport delivers the most gains, and forget that *no one thing is right all the time, for everyone*. But we can't resist the urge to place things in rank order, and in doing so we ruin our relationship with them by entering into a competition that can't be won.

A starting point for feeling compassion towards our own bodies and movement preferences is to remember that we are practising confirmation bias in relation to our bodies when we compare ourselves only with those *who look like us*. If we broaden our view and appreciate that the body of nature to which we inextricably belong is far more diverse than ourselves, we can begin to *re-imagine* how our own bodies might fit into the wider world. Instead of seeing our bodies – and by extension ourselves – as outliers that don't belong – featuring too much of this or too little of that – we can imagine ourselves as yet another beautiful, idiosyncratic expression of nature's wish to re-generate and live.

Nature is profoundly non-judgemental. It doesn't care how you look, what you wear, what speed you move at, the colour of your skin, the size of your body, it's capability. It doesn't discern or treat you any differently however you are. We have made each

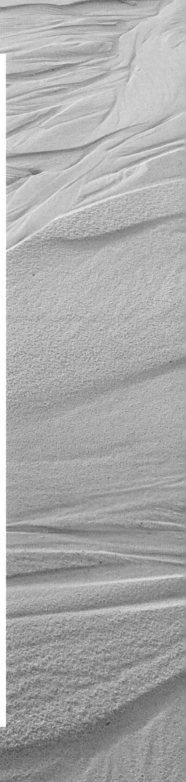

STAND LIKE A MOUNTAIN

A great question to ask yourself at any time is, *'What do I want to embody?'* Today, you may want to embody confidence, tomorrow gentleness – or courage, assertiveness, kindness, fearlessness. In order to become more grounded, stability, strength, calmness, balance and measure are just a few qualities that you may wish to embody.

Tadasana or 'Mountain pose' in yoga is a very simple stance, but it forms a foundational position of strength from which many other standing movements flow.

1. Stand with your feet together, big toes touching. You will probably have to turn out your heels a bit. Face your kneecaps over your toes.
2. Your weight should be evenly distributed between each foot. To check this, ground down, lift your kneecaps, and engage your quadriceps muscles. Press the backs of your knees forward without bending but engaging your quads and hamstring muscles equally. Hug your upper thighs together, then press them away from one another to activate your inner and outer thighs.
3. With your arms alongside your body, turn your biceps and palms to face forward. Align your neck so it feels long and even on all sides.
4. Take a deep breath inward and lift your rib cage away from your pelvis; exhale and hug in the sides of your waist to create lower back stability.
5. Stay in this position for as long as you need to feel grounded.

other unequal, nature hasn't. Your unique movement pattern and signature, the way *you do you in your body,* has a place. That place is here on the ground on which you live and accepting the way that you are in your glorious, natural, diversity, is a way of becoming grounded within yourself and within the rest of the world.

BECOMING EMBODIED

The way *you do you in your body* can be called 'embodiment'. Living in your body with an awareness that it is yours, and that you *are* your body, is also embodiment. That you have definable and observable limits that are breakable, can be pushed, can be surpassed (and are also unsurpassable) is also embodiment. Seeing your body as 'I' not 'it' is embodiment: it is where the line blurs between the body as object, and the body as subject. Being wholly, ordinarily alive is embodiment. Embodied is what we are as humans, whether we like it or not, because even when we are not aware of it, we are living in our bodies. The power of embodiment grows when we become aware and come home to ourselves in our bodies. When we become, as somatic therapist Christine Caldwell calls it, '*bodyful'.*

Becoming more embodied through awareness and movement (and awareness of what moves in and through you) is one of the great goals and rewards of becoming grounded. It can help us live more confidently, happily and healthily, and through becoming aware of our lived experience in the body we realize almost all things are tolerable, bearable, workable, survivable. It also feels good for its own sake. Moving on from a starting point of compassion, becoming embodied in ourselves is an important step on the journey back to ourselves as grounded humans in the world.

It's not, however, a word to get hung up on, or something to worry about 'doing right'. You are already embodied by virtue of being alive in a body. In many ways, embodiment is nothing special; it is mundane and ordinary. It is up to you to make it exciting and extraordinary – and this is easier when you really connect with how exciting it is to move your body with awareness outdoors, where the rest of nature is also moving, breathing, living. The ability, shape, age, colour of your body should not be a barrier to you going outside. There are many ways to become more consciously embodied, one of which is to reclaim movement.

RECLAIMING MOVEMENT

If we understand that movement is life, then we can also recognize that movement is not about calorie burning, body shaping, goal-achieving or simple athleticism. All of these things may really work for you, but none of them encompass the true essence of movement. Moving is about being alive; and being alive is about vitality, reducing suffering, embracing joy (among many other things).

If we cannot separate movement from achievement, then we will be shackled to the idea that movement should look and feel a certain way, that it is perhaps a punishment, that it is something to *suffer*. Movement is about finding a way of being in your body that is joyful, nourishing, supportive, caring, confident, agentic. It is about something that feels good for you and that supports your sense of 'aliveness' or vitality.

We also need to recognize that our movement needs may change over time or in different situations. Walking is a go-to movement for many of us, though not for all. For others it will be spinning the wheels of their chair, or their bike, or a partner on the dance floor. Some will swear by yoga and others will swear never to do it again. Sometimes you will run because you like to; sometimes you will hate it. Today you might slump around for twenty minutes because you can't be bothered, tomorrow you might ride for hours. You might triathlon. You might ultra. You might stretch. You might bobsleigh. You might practise for your black belt. Tai-chi. Parkour. Parkrun. Do the gardening.

When movement is life and it is happening everywhere, then you can take your pick of the options for moving. Overcoming inertia is always the hardest part.

Whatever you choose, listen to your intuition. Intuitive movement is about giving your body what it wants and needs through tuning into your body's sensations. What would you like to do today? Where can you feel tension in your body that you could attend to? Asking yourself questions about what you are drawn to, and giving yourself answers with an interest in the 'Why?' is a simple way of getting to know your body more fully, becoming embodied, becoming grounded.

> **Movement is about finding a way of being in your body that is joyful, nourishing, supportive, caring, confident, agentic.**

EXERCISE NATURALLY

Next time you're exercising, consider integrating jumping, squatting, crawling and lifting into your routine. Many practitioners also encourage you to try these movements barefoot and outside in a natural environment for maximum benefit. If the weather is suitable, why not find somewhere pleasant and clean to walk barefoot and see how it feels. Alternatively, stay inside and get playful. The living room floor is the perfect place to do a bit of stretching, crawling and squatting without anyone else seeing. As you get braver, head out to a local woodland and do some jumping around using natural obstacles like fallen trees, branches and puddles. It's a lot of fun and being more playful is great for our wellbeing too.

NATURAL MOVEMENT

In recent years, there has been a resurgent interest in *natural movement*. Definitions and systems abound, but it can be simply understood as movements that are in 'accordance with nature'. As humans are part of nature, this can be anything that the human body is able to do, or does do, in order to *function,* such as walking, climbing, lifting, or catching. Practitioners of natural movement encourage us all to move in a variety of ways that are natural for our strength, flexibility, function and overall wellbeing, but which we may have forgotten over the centuries as we have moved indoors and become sedentary for long periods.

THE BENEFITS OF MOVING OUTSIDE

Movement, wherever you do it, will be beneficial, but taking it outside adds a holistic dimension. Research suggests that physical activity undertaken in a natural environment provides greater synergistic benefits than either regular indoor exercise or contact with nature alone. So-called 'green exercise' has the grounding benefits of enhancing mood and self-esteem, can reduce blood pressure and burn calories, and often facilitates social connection at the same time. Mixing up different types of exercise in different habitats has also been found to be beneficial. And the best news of all – the greatest benefits were found to occur in the first five minutes of exercise. After that, you can simply enjoy the views knowing that good things are happening while you move.

Of course, before gyms and other purpose-built indoor facilities, exercising outdoors would have been the norm. Taking movement outside is nothing new but perhaps something we need to remember to do more, scheduling it into our week when we can. Outside you don't just get exercise, but you feel the weather on your body, experience the sights and sounds of nature, and see other life in movement. The question is not why take movement outside, but why wouldn't you?

STILLNESS THROUGH MOVEMENT

Achieving stillness in nature is not just about standing or sitting without moving. Moving about in nature can also create a sense of inner stillness or quiet. The process of moving can be highly relaxing, enabling us to tap into the meditative qualities of nature, in the same manner as sitting still. Through movement, the jangly, stressed energy of the day can be discharged, and we can become quite mindful, letting thoughts come and go, with the only focus being the movement itself. This is a different way of being still in nature, when being externally motionless feels too hard to achieve. Sitting still is not for everyone; and sometimes sitting with our feelings in a mindful way is too overwhelming, or brings up too much emotion to deal with. In these cases, moving outside in nature can be a far more accessible and less overwhelming way of accessing inner stillness and a break from the internal noise.

MOVEMENT IN MIND

Gaining greater awareness of how the movement of our mind – our mental activity – affects us, and how this can be focused and grounded is also key to wellbeing. We can learn to gently notice the movement that happens inside us – the physical sensations, emotions (e.g. feelings of being stuck, doubt, worry) – as a means of getting in touch with ourselves and becoming more grounded through self-awareness.

Once we acknowledge what's going on, it becomes possible to track movements in terms of intensity and longevity, and then to notice, act on, or simply to watch with curiosity, the thoughts and sensations.

Feelings, thoughts and moods are like the weather: they come and go. Often, they will blow through us and transform into something else if we watch for long enough. Attaching to anything in particular can be unhelpful, but times of bad weather can be destructive if we don't simply let it run its course, without pressure or judgement. Attaching too heavily is akin to hugging a storm. Following our most negative feelings often leads to further despair. We are sometimes wiser to take cover, keep safe and emerge when the winds have settled. What lies beyond is clearer sky. From here, there is often improved clarity and we can make better choices for ourselves.

JUST WALK

As humans, we like to make things complicated and having made life very complex, we can be sceptical about simple things having any benefit. However, walking is one of the simplest ways you can move into a better state of wellness. The holistic benefits of walking, even for fifteen minutes a day, have been well documented in recent years:

- Walking outside in good daylight boosts Vitamin D, which many of us are deficient in but has a natural anti-depressant effect.
- Walking lowers levels of the stress hormone cortisol in your body and interrupts the parts of your brain associated with sadness and rumination.
- Walking helps you feel grounded and provides a means of gaining inner stillness and its rhythmic movements have meditative benefits.

Try different types of walking for specific benefits, from the mindfulness of slow, attentive walks, via the life-changing power of long-distance walking, through to the philosophical benefits of simply wandering and getting lost.

SPOT INNER WEATHER PATTERNS

Investing time in thinking about how you think – the features of your prevailing mental 'weather system' – is time well spent. By noticing which thoughts you focus on, and which you don't, you can determine how mental energy – movement – flows through the system. Awareness brings an element of choice, agency, and opportunity to become more grounded – would you rather move into good feelings, or into bad?

Consider keeping a 'weather diary' of your moods a few times a day over the course of a week. Instead of labelling each mood as 'happy' or 'sad', try using a more descriptive weather metaphor. Note the nuances in your mood in the same way as you might explain the weather outside. This might enable you to track and observe your short, medium and long-range forecast. It might help you see that things pass and if they don't, perhaps this is when you need to seek help.

When we can spot our own weather patterns, and become more aware of what comes and goes, then we can accommodate ourselves accordingly, supporting ourselves more at times when we might predict we will need more love and care.

AUDIT YOUR LIFE ECOLOGY

In order to support your own sustainable sense of vitality, it's important to consider the whole environment or 'ecology' of your life. Put another way, does the 'set up' of your life support an overall sense of aliveness and wellbeing? You could start by asking yourself the following questions:

- Are you commuting long hours? If so, what do you need to do to minimize the physical and mental impact?
- Are you moving enough throughout the day?
- How much time do you spend in artificial environments?
- Are you making healthy choices with your food and drink?
- Are you getting enough sleep?
- Do you give yourself time to relax and switch off?
- Are you mindful about the time and content of your media consumption and how it leaves you feeling?
- What about your relationships? Are the connections in your life meaningful and supportive?

This might sound daunting, but it needn't be. All you need to do is keep an eye on the things that you might not usually consider as having an effect, understanding that every choice we make has the potential to support or diminish our wellbeing and sense of grounding. Nature teaches us that everything is connected and needs attending to if we are to be 'healthy'. Why not take a half an hour in the next week to give yourself a gentle, whole-system, wellbeing audit.

STILLNESS

THE ESSENCE OF STILLNESS

Stillness is a break. It is also a pause. It is the white space around words, and the rest between notes of music. It doesn't need to be anything more than this. But stillness is also a place to complete our ideas and finish our thoughts, a place to sift through our memories and craft insight from our experiences. Sometimes it is 'the absence of', other times it is 'the fullness of'. In any case, it is a contained state of its own that is at once about going nowhere while inviting us to go *somewhere*.

When I am churned-up, agitated, stressed or in any other way *busy* within myself, I find it hard to give others my best attention. I make a lot of effort to enter into a state of stillness before being with someone in the counselling space, because this is how I become quiet enough within myself to really *listen* and notice what's happening to the person sitting in front of me or walking beside me. Stillness allows me to bracket what I don't need to feel at that moment, in order to make space to feel what the other person is experiencing. Cultivating stillness in this way is something I try and do in the moments before I begin

working, but it is also something I make space for every day. I am trying to become habitually still, and the best method for me is to go outside to a quiet place and be quiet myself. When I can become still, I sometimes feel as if I can hear the whole universe talking.

In a talk by Pico Iyer, he provides a useful description of stillness. In stillness, he explains, we develop more attentive and appreciative eyes. In stillness we can ask ourselves if we are content, and if not why. In the din and clamour of our increasingly 'on-demand lives', stillness offers us a fighting chance of catching up with ourselves. Stillness is the antidote that we need to rest and replenish from our hyper-busy connectedness, so that we don't lose contact with ourselves.

As finite beings, time is one of the most precious commodities we have, but all too often we squander it in pursuit of productivity. Gently, generously, stillness hands our time back to us. Gratefully we receive it, knowing that empty space is a luxury. Somehow, stillness softens the edges of noise, giving it a different shape and beauty, making it more tolerable, or perhaps even energizing. Quietly, we become aware of our own breath, or another's breath. In this way, stillness is one of the most intimate ways of being.

STILLNESS IN NATURE

We can quieten down and be still anywhere and there will be value in it. Stillness does not require us to go outside, but to access the grounding benefits of nature we *are* sometimes required to be still and quiet. Modern, urbanized environments operate at a different sound level to nature, often drowning out the ambient tones of what the natural environment has to offer. Quietening down is a way of making ourselves available to natural sounds and of becoming more attuned to the frequency and pitch of their communication. What fills the stillness in a wild, more natural place is different to what fills stillness indoors. Different sounds and sights activate the senses outside, and you do not as much invite silence (although this is also possible in certain places) as make space for a different way of sensing the world around you.

Stillness in nature provides a chance to listen to the wind in the trees, or the water breaking on a shore, or the rustle of leaves. When you are quiet, birds become louder and their distress calls may turn to song. In stillness, there is time to take note of the smells of nature and to engage your sense of touch. Sitting still on a rock, you are invited to feel the texture and temperature of things that are almost immoveable. At the water's edge, being still is time to dangle your arms and legs in the water and let them be cooled and moved without effort.

Often when I sit still indoors, it is a struggle to quieten the internal chatter of my busy mind. When I go outdoors, I don't have to try so hard: nature fills the space and I can more easily relinquish the persistent thoughts of things I need to do, chores I need to finish, the endless overturning of things I do or don't know. I can also step away from the buzzing of technology, the hyper-colour world of social media, the news and the internet in general. Instead, I can be with nature and become conscious of what nature *knows* – and what nature knows is how to simply rest in *being*. It is not busy with trying to be what it is or isn't: it just *is*. Few things are as grounded as a rock.

GROUNDING THROUGH STILLNESS

Stillness in nature can provide us with opportunities for grounding that differ from those given by movement. While movement offers the mover a chance to release energy that might be making it hard to settle into stillness and introduces a figurative movement into problems that might be keeping us agitated and restless, *being still* invites a time to just *be* with what is from the outset, turning our attention to what is on the outside as well as the inside. Stillness through movement begins as a busier process, stillness in nature as a deliberate slowing.

THE BENEFITS OF STILLNESS IN NATURE

There are a variety of ways in which we can both absorb and reflect the benefits of the stillness that can be found in nature. These calming, grounding processes restore body and mind and give us the space to think more clearly and find focus.

Inner spaciousness

Being still, quietening our body and the inner chatter of our mind, is a way of *making space* within ourselves. It is a way of being empty that is restful and useful. Nature can be a great aide in creating inner spaciousness because it provides visual cues and metaphors that show us what spaciousness looks like and how it feels.

Sitting on the shore looking out to sea, we quickly become aware of the vast expanse of water and the persistent but distant horizon. Spending time contemplating an unbroken expanse of blue is one way that we can internalize a feeling of inner spaciousness; breathing in the sea and imagining it *within us* is a way of embodying the feeling of expansiveness. The same is true when we observe any natural panorama, but particularly those with a homogenous quality such as oceans, deserts, mountains ranging as far as the eye can see, or blankets of forest seen from above. In this way, outside spaces become a mirror for the space we want to create inside.

These feelings are harder to replicate indoors when we are contained within a far smaller (perhaps more cluttered) space. When we are outdoors with plenty of space around us, we can come to know what expansiveness *feels* like inside, because we are experiencing it outside.

The sense of having inner space is a good feeling – a restful antidote to our normal, often messy, lives. But inner stillness can also be a place of unfolding. In stillness, we can think things through if we want to, we can be with what arises in us, we can move around within our emotions. With stillness and space, we can work out what it is we feel and what it is we want to do next. As Pema Chödrön reminds us, 'Once we've touched in with spaciousness it begins to permeate everything. Once we've had a glimpse of spaciousness, it will continue to expand. It expands into our resentment. It expands into our fear. It expands into our concepts and opinions about things and into who we think we are'. In a noisy and demanding world, stillness and spaciousness helps us separate the signal from the noise. Spaciousness allows for resonance; it helps us to perceive the world and notice what chimes with us. Spaciousness is clarifying and the home of emotional intelligence. Within it is a stabilizing sense of infinity.

By tapping into nature's inherent peacefulness, we can become quiet and still enough to truly find where our contentment lies.

Peacefulness

Peace and quiet go hand-in-hand. Stillness, and its associated quality of quietness, is the counterpoint to movement, energy and stress. Even if we are not *feeling stressed,* the fact of being in movement requires an expenditure of energy that often generates or invites noise – literal and internal – and can be a way of being busy and active, rather than still or quiet.

When we slow down, quietness descends, and this is as vital for our wellbeing as doing things. This is why time spent in peaceful places is good for us. When resting, our parasympathetic nervous system is activated and repair happens. The same positive impact on our bodies and minds – the stimulation of our 'rest and digest' parasympathetic response – has been shown to occur when we spend quiet, still time in a forest.

Such calm, wild places also soften our emotional responses, helping us to gain a sense of tranquillity. The writer Wendell Berry beautifully describes this in his poetic masterpiece 'The Peace of Wild Things'. Nature quietly going about its business shows us how to be peaceful. Watching birds glide effortlessly on glassy water, observing the gentlest of breezes move through

USE SOFT FASCINATION

One of the most significant theories about how time spent in nature benefits human wellbeing was developed by Stephen and Rachel Kaplan in the 1980s. They hypothesized that nature improves our focus and ability to concentrate and reduces mental fatigue by restoring the normal function and ability that existed before our busy, noisy, hyper-connected, technicolour lives made us distractable, ultra-vigilant and stressed out.

They explained that the restoration of our minds happens most effectively when we get away from what is fatiguing us (physically or psychologically) into environments that feel good and comfortable, and which we have chosen through personal motivation. Places where we can turn gentle attention – or soft fascination – towards the world around us.

To practise soft fascination, try adopting a passive, less active way of noticing. Instead of focusing *hard* on whatever is in front of you, to the extent that you are completely absorbed, try to just reflect or 'float' around the experience. You can try this activity indoors as well as outside:

1. Gently focus your eyes on a chosen feature (perhaps a tree, rock, hillside if you're outside, or a plant, piece of furniture, window inside) near to you.
2. Now float your eyes across the landscape or room, moving on and not settling to focus on anything in particular, as if you had glazed eyes.
3. Allow your mind to drift into a state of reflection and introspection.

long grass, noticing a barely breaking wave. All of these things are peaceful. What brings you a sense of peace may be unique and idiosyncratic, but there is surely something universal about sitting in a wetland bird hide on a white-washed, no-weather day watching all sorts of species come and go, dipping in and out of the water, lounging on the banks and twitching the reeds.

Observing the peacefulness of nature encourages us to replicate this quality in ourselves. It tells us something about simplicity, harmony and the balance of noise and sound. It is hard to be peaceful when we feel agitated, stressed or overburdened. Nature being itself, shows us how to do just enough, but no more than that. It shows us that calm isn't achieved without movement, but by having everything in its right place at the right time. It is things being just as they are, without a fuss. By tapping into nature's inherent peacefulness, we can become quiet and still enough to truly find where our contentment lies.

WAYS TO BE STILL IN NATURE

Becoming quiet and still doesn't require us to do much more than exactly that. While movement requires the use of energy, stillness demands a lot less from us. There is no special way or secret, no equipment needed and no training required. The biggest challenge in achieving stillness is making space for it in the first place. The unobtrusive quality of stillness means that we are far more likely to forget about it than we are to make a noise or stay busy.

Set the intention

Doing less ought to be less effort, but of course sometimes doing less requires more will than simply carrying on with doing more. This is the nature of our busy lives. The best way we can hold space for stillness is by setting the intention to do so, committing to giving it time, and simply doing it. As if we're on a plane coming in to land, we can prepare ourselves by putting away the things we are doing, turning off electrical items and getting comfortable so that our bodies come into rest. This preparation is something that we can do while walking to a quiet place in nature. I recommend a rock in the mountains, a quiet spot among the trees, or at the water's edge.

Explore with the senses

One practical way of becoming still and tuning in to nature's language is to quieten down our internal noise and to enter into a mindful and multisensory exploration of what's around us. This involves turning our attention to our external surroundings and consciously engaging *all* of our senses, rather than those we use by default – for many of us, this is primarily sight. To embark on a multi-sensory exploration of nature is to become alive to how nature feels to the touch, how it smells, how it sounds and, when safe to do so, how it tastes. Exploring in this sensory way brings nature into focus and can distance us from our thoughts for a while. Sometimes when we are busy in our own head, we can charge through a landscape and all of its detail is lost in a hurt, angry, anxious, worried, excitable fog. By switching off from our thoughts and diverting attention to our senses we can come into contact and connection with nature again and become internally still, even if we are moving.

Experiencing nature in this way might reveal things that you would have otherwise overlooked: if you follow smell

GET YOUR HANDS DIRTY

One of the easiest and most accessible ways in which to explore the earth in a more sensory way is to literally put your hands into it and *feel* what our living planet is made of. Not only will the texture feel good and soothing, possibly even energizing, in its own right (once you have got over the peculiarly adult aversion to getting 'needlessly' muddy), but microbes found in soil are thought to have an anti-depressant effect, inducing an immune response that increases serotonin levels in the brain.

You may have noticed how good fresh soil smells in a damp woodland or when you're gardening. A very easy way of getting in touch with the texture of earth is to do some planting in a garden or in containers. Planting is life-affirming, life-giving and confidence-building – there's a reason why horticultural therapy is well established and allotments are so popular. If you find you love having contact with soil but don't have access to garden space, containers or an allotment, try looking for a local community garden where you can increase your social connectivity at the same time.

rather than sight, you are likely to end up in a very different place to where your eyes might have led you. A multi-sensory journey into nature can reinvigorate us by connecting us with what is really around us, but often ignored. In this sort of stillness, where human noise is reduced, we are reminded of our place in the natural world: we move from 'I' to 'we'. Inner stillness is created through a mindful presence or 'being with' what is around us, whether we are sitting still, or quietly and gently moving around.

> **A multi-sensory journey into nature can reinvigorate us by connecting us with what is really around us, but often ignored.**

Be mindful

Practising nature-based mindfulness can also make us feel more present and grounded. Observing our thoughts, feelings and sensations as we pass through a natural environment, connecting with it and with ourselves, we can tap into the wisdom offered by nature and use it to find solutions.

Becoming mindful in nature is about noticing what is in front of you in the present, with all your available senses. Noticing what you can see, hear, smell, touch and even taste (if appropriate) are all ways of becoming more aware of what is with you in the moment. There is no special way to be mindful in nature but rather than rushing somewhere, gently letting go of the things on your mind, other than that which is in front of you, walking at a gentle meditative pace in a place where you can turn your attention to nature are simple ways to become more mindful. At the heart of this kind of mindful engagement with nature is being with – noticing what you might not usually have time or space to notice down to the tiniest details. This goes for what is happening outside of you and inside. By shifting your attention both inwards and outwards at intervals, you can work mindfully with both the outer and inner landscape.

Seek silence

'Silence is the only language spacious enough to include everything' is the profound observation of Franciscan friar Richard Rohr. Silence is also increasingly hard to find. Few environments are truly silent, whether man-made or natural. Outdoor habitats that teem with life are not especially silent, yet many people (myself included) head outside in pursuit of silence anyway, trying to get as close as they can to an absolute absence of noise. Over the years I have had

PRACTISE MINDFUL PHOTOGRAPHY

One practical way of engaging and connecting with nature is to practise mindful photography. In this form of contemplation, the aim is to really take time to notice what you are drawn to, and to be present in the moment with your camera rather than focused on 'getting the right shot'. Mindful photography is about making the effort to see the detail in front of you and giving the natural world your attention for a while.

This slower, purposeful approach to picture taking will allow you to consciously shut out the worries and preoccupations of your mind. It also provides a structure for spending more time outside and noticing what's around you, grounding you in the present moment and connecting you with the living planet.

In time, you may want to experiment with using mindful photography to take pictures that capture your thoughts, feelings and emotions in the present moment. This is a different way of connecting with nature, where you are seeking metaphors within the living landscape as a means of accessing your own emotional world. This can be a great way of discovering more about yourself without needing to find the words. The better we know ourselves, the easier it is to feel grounded and settled in our minds and bodies.

moderate success, finding moments of the most profound and beautiful silence imaginable on sheltered mountain slopes, or deep within the snowy forests of the far north. But these precious moments are fleeting and often broken by the wind, or by my own shifting and coughing. Even a slowed heartbeat buried under layers of clothing can shatter silence.

Moments of silence are by necessity moments of stillness. The quietness is emptying, ecstatic and sometimes painful. Like perfect snowflakes, they are glimmers of something almost sacred. They cannot be held or accurately described, as is fitting for something divinely rare, but they can be profound. Anyone who has experienced the gentle, muffling quality of falling or settled snow, will know the power of this type of silence on a tired, bereaved or anxious mind.

What many of us are looking for when we head out in pursuit of silence is actually quietness, and a break from human-generated noise. We may not be expecting silence at all, but the ambient and soothing noise of nature that is restorative to the modern mind. Nature doesn't even have to be *that quiet* to work its magic. A waterfall and the dawn chorus will wake many sleepers before

Noticing beauty is about becoming aware of the little things all around us, wherever we are.

they are ready, but the quality of the sound is different to the noise we generate ourselves, and this is often a relief.

The interesting truth of silence is that it exists because of sound. The two are ontologically related and rely on each other. Without sound we can't have silence, and without noise we wouldn't have or appreciate quietness. Our challenge then is to appreciate and balance the presence of both within our lives – noticing the times when we need one over the other and giving ourselves what we need.

Notice beauty

It's easy to forget, but the world is full of beauty. From the smallest world-mirroring dew drop to the star-strung sky. Staying still and paying attention for long enough to notice what is beautiful in the natural world is an important way of connecting with nature and the possibility of goodness and positivity in our lives. Noting what is beautiful and what we are grateful for in nature strengthens our relationship with the natural world and in turn supports our own wellbeing through the development of positive emotion. Various studies show that wellbeing is increased in individuals who *perceive* themselves to be in areas that contain

KEEP A BEAUTIFUL NATURE DIARY

Noticing beauty may generate new neural pathways that provoke optimistic action. Researcher Laura Sewall calls us to be 'saturated by the generous beauty of the natural order' so that we might change our despairing, stuck brains for the better. It's worth remembering that beauty is in the eye of the beholder. What is remarkable and worthy of note, what brings you to a place of awe, might be entirely unique: there are no rules, and no absolute truth. It's important to find what speaks to you and to find ways to keep yourself open to it in your daily life. Keep a 'beautiful nature' diary over the course of a few months; note a few things every day and see what happens.

diverse birds, butterflies and plants, particularly when these are found to be close to home. Moreover, noticing beauty every day for a month has been shown to elicit a sustained connection with nature, which we know improves wellbeing.

Noticing beauty is about becoming aware of the little things all around us, wherever we are. The smallest flower can be a jolt of beauty in an otherwise over-developed urban unit, so too can the way the light falls between an avenue of urban trees. Frost-touched spiderwebs; shoaling fish; ants carrying leaf cuttings.

It requires no special effort to seek out beauty – when we are open to it, beauty simply arrives and flows into the spaces that need it: we only need to tune in. Tuning in to the smallest of beautiful things in nature is a way of retraining our minds to seek things that are good and affirming and can help us to develop a positive world view. It can

be helpful when we have slipped into negative thought patterns or have started to feel that there's no goodness left in the world, or when we are tired of the urban environment and feel that there is no nature available to us. Nature shows us that there *is*, if we can just quieten down and notice what's been there all along.

We live in difficult times, when our planet is being destroyed and the damage is real and undeniable. To protect and advocate for it, we have to first believe that doing so is still worthwhile. Reconnecting with beauty through mindful stillness, and stimulating wonder and awe is one way in which we can remind ourselves that all is not lost. There is much of value that needs our love and care, just as we need it. In this way, noticing the beauty in nature deeply connects us with it, promotes positive emotions, and invites us to become purposeful in protecting everything that is beautiful in the world.

FIND FRACTALS

There is so much to be admired in the flowing, soft-sided, chaotic body of nature when we step away from the linear, hard-edged urban world of our own creation and, the truth is, we have an eye for it.

Repeating, branching, patterns in nature – also known as 'fractals' – are found in everything from snowflakes and broccoli to ammonite fossils, trees and floodplains. Our attraction to these beautiful, natural patterns is well-established, but a recent study by physicist Professor Richard Taylor has shown that we love fractals because they have a 'visual fluency' that fits with the structure of the human eye. Buildings and other man-made structures do not share this visual fluency, and so we find it harder to process their aesthetics. In short, we find fractals relaxing, soothing, de-stressing.

For a quick green fix, enjoy the soothing properties of fractals by finding pictures of deltas, canyons, plant leaves, lightning and all sorts of other natural fractals online. When you have more time, find them outside. I am pretty sure that the visual flow of ferns is why we love these plants so much!

SOLITUDE

THE VALUE OF SOLITUDE

There is a tree on a hill that I love. It's a long walk to the tree, but as the path opens out into the broad glacial valley ahead of me, I catch sight of it. In a hurry, I move quickly and excitedly. *I'm back.* Every time I meet the tree again, I am caught by a feeling of recognition. I am struck by its wind-swept location, its apparent isolation, its seasonal predicament; depending on my mood, I will see great strength in that tree, or I will feel a deep sadness for it.

The solitary tree offers me a mirror on my own emotional state and is a barometer of my inner weather. And while it is one of my favourite solitary trees, it is not the only one. Noticing solitary trees is something I do a lot. Solitude in nature is readily observable, and the pull towards solitude is readily observable in me.

When we talk to each other, we are not alone, although it may be true that we feel lonely. Therapy is often full of silences when a person is alone with their thoughts. I have always considered these moments to be powerful – and there is a fine balance to be struck in deciding whether to ask to be allowed *in,* or to wait on the other side of the silence until thoughts are shared, or the conversation moves on. Outdoors, these snippets of solitude in therapy take on a different tone. When both people are silent, the rest of nature is often more audible and visible, and we may get caught in a moment of being with what's happening in nature, rather than with each other. These moments can be very rich, and an important part of the conversation that resumes afterwards. Moments of solitude in therapy are possible and can be very valuable; this is no surprise to me because being alone is integral to life and may be essential in the journey to becoming more grounded.

BEING ALONE IS PART OF LIFE

When we stand on the ground and look down, we see our own feet. We can see our own outline, notice the boundary of skin or clothing that marks the physical extent of ourselves, and the presence of everything that is outside of us. Patting our hips, thighs and down the length of our legs, we can feel the solid boundary of our body. We can call this our *container.*

There is an inherent element of self-containment in being alive in the world, expressed neatly through the limit of the body, which on the whole keeps the stuff of us inside, and the rest of the world outside. This is one way of being alone that is thrust upon us from the time that our cells come together to form us, and it is reinstated for a second time when we are born and enter the world as a whole body unto ourselves. We are reliant on our caregivers of course, but we are also inherently separate from the very beginning, and the push and pull of this earliest separation stays with us for as long as we live.

Being alone is integral to life and may be essential in the journey to becoming more grounded.

This is the ongoing challenge – to be with others (because to lesser and greater extents, we are all governed by an ongoing proximity to others), while also managing the inevitability of being alone with ourselves. Our paradox lies in being a discrete entity in a populated, interconnected world and a relationship-seeking creature in a disconnected, often geographically uprooted world. Being, or feeling, alone at various points in our lives is an inevitability, and many would say loneliness is part of the human condition. Practising solitude can allow us to find value in being alone, making it restful, creative, stabilizing and reparative.

SOLITUDE IN NATURE

Solitude is the state or quality of being alone. It is the time that we spend physically away from others *and* the time we spend in the proximity to others without contact, connection or communication. Inner and outer solitude can be found while walking alone, in silent retreat with others, or in the isolation of sleep. In these moments we are more fully in the space of ourselves – in the vessel that houses us until the end. It has a weight of its own and a composition of seen and unseen, felt and unfelt parts.

Choosing to be alone outdoors, whether it's walking, swimming or running – whatever it is that feels necessary – when I *could* be in company is one way that I practise solitude. I devise my own plans, set my own agenda, move at my own pace and do it all so quietly that I can hear the world outside and in. I let my time unfold without demand. Alone, I notice the thoughts passing through my mind, the sensations in my body, I note when my energy levels surge and dissolve, I listen for the richness in silence. Nothing is ignored.

Time outside, immersed in nature, offers an unparalleled opportunity to be alone and away from other humans. The degree of *true* solitude you experience, and the degree of comfort you reject or embrace, is up to you. Solitude can be found in a hammock strung between two trees on a sunny summer's afternoon, swaying in a soft breeze and listening to gentle birdsong. It can also be found in a wind-blown tent, straining at its poles, on a remote mountainside far from civilization. It can be discovered in the corner of a busy urban park, or while waiting to catch a wave out at sea. For some people, being alone will be most revealing – and educational or enlightening – at the point at which they are under the greatest mental, emotional or physical strain. For others, this is too much, and sitting quietly observing fish in a pond is more than enough.

Outside, there are plenty of distractions that make solitude bearable, even enjoyable.

Whatever your preference, natural spaces offer somewhere to be alone, while never being entirely alone. Sitting alone in a room has a different quality to sitting on a bench with a view of a landscape. The former is likely to be quieter and feel more contained; the whole sensory experience is likely to be reduced. Outside, there are plenty of

distractions that make solitude bearable, even enjoyable. Without people, we are more likely to notice the wildlife in our local environment; we are more likely to notice the flavour and tone of the weather; the soundscape – natural or otherwise – and a hundred and one other details that in someone else's company we might overlook while enjoying human *togetherness*.

THE PARADOX OF SOLITUDE

Everything in nature is alone but connected: interconnected. Even a lone wolf, loping through empty miles of unbroken snow will eventually come across a pack, meet its prey, or at the very least be observed by another living creature in hiding or from up above.

In relation to the rest of nature, we are forever *a part* and *apart*. The paradox of solitude is that we can seek time alone but, in various ways, we will always be in contact with the rest of the world. If we go out into nature, then we are away from our own species but closer to others – alone from the human world but never entirely alone from the other-than-human. Escaping to a cabin in the woods, we are still in the company of trees. While it is true that we are separated from the rest of nature by having a spoken language and a different cognitive processor, we have also separated ourselves from nature through our treatment of the world. Yet we can still come back and seek communion and connection: the rest of nature does not bear a grudge.

When we spend our time outside with other people, our gazes and words fix more easily on our companions and it is easy to forget that we can connect with the rest of the world. If we go outside alone, togetherness takes on a different meaning. It is no longer restricted to being with humans but encompasses the other-than-human world: what is there becomes our acquaintance and our fellowship.

The fact that it is almost impossible to think of a situation in which we could ever be *entirely* alone, because of the presence of the rest of nature, is an invitation to those who are anxious about solitude to find comfort in being alone. Humans may bring certain relational qualities that other species cannot, but the gap is perhaps not as wide as you might imagine. It is possible to feel allegiance with other animals, and safety in our environment. Company does not always require the verbal element of communication, and there is solace in the sheer presence of life, human or otherwise.

GOOD ACTIVITIES TO DO ALONE IN NATURE

1. Take a walk alone and stop more than you might do with someone else. Take your time. On your own there is no need to rush to please anyone else.
2. Get involved: look more closely, pick things up, smell things; do things that might feel awkward in front of another person!
3. Listen to nature: this is difficult when someone else is talking next to you.
4. Make a creative study of things that interest you: spend a few hours outside making a photographic catalogue of something you are attracted to, or do some drawing, sketching or painting of natural things.
5. Visit a botanical garden or nature reserve. Here you can be by yourself but also feel the comfort of being near others who are interested in spending their day in a similar way.

DON'T BE AFRAID OF SOLITUDE

We are everywhere. As a species we are present in so many places, and digitally linked when we are not. One of the great losses of our hyper-connected lives is that many of us have forgotten how to be alone, or even that it is *possible* and might hold any value. Those pockets of time that used to lie idle in our day are often now filled with scrolling on our phones, or mindlessly flicking through the same apps and webpages on repeat. Where once a period of downtime was a chance to daydream or play, we are now more inclined to use it for things that keep us in some way connected with others, even if the link is tenuous and unfulfilling. We have reduced our tolerance for *being with ourselves,* and perhaps have even become avoidant of ourselves. In turn, we have begun to fear solitude, fear ourselves when we're alone, and fear what the world has to offer us if we are alone.

Being alone, even for a short time, and especially outside, has become unsafe in the minds of many. We are warned of the risks of catastrophic isolation and bottomless depression, the risk of physical harm if no one is there to protect us. At worst, we are told that the world wishes us harm: that a poor outcome is inevitable. If you take sensible precautions, there is nothing inherently fearful or risky about being alone.

Solitude versus loneliness

Being 'alone' is emotionally charged. How you feel about it will depend on your experience. For some, being alone is something to enjoy, relish and seek; if you ask such people 'Would you like some time alone?', they will jump at it, eyes lit and ready to go, as if you had offered them the most precious finite resource. For others, spending time alone is something to be suffered or avoided, and they will greet the suggestion with a groan, suggesting impending misery or even total annihilation. Your perception of others' experiences – whether they have had a damaging time alone or, conversely, have been inspiringly productive – will also influence your view. Either way, the concept of being alone rarely invites indifference.

This polarization can be explained by how we label our experience of time alone. 'Solitude' and 'loneliness' reflecting the *joy* and *pain* of being alone, respectively. Both are available to us; the ongoing challenge of spending time alone is how to navigate the tension between them. Too much time alone can dissolve into loneliness, so too can

isolation that is forced upon us, perhaps through the ending of a relationship, ill-health or bereavement. Not having any time to ourselves, however, can leave us stressed, overwhelmed and wrung-out by others. The challenge of solitude is not to tip over into loneliness.

Well-managed solitude has the power to restore our minds and bodies, whereas loneliness diminishes both. Being able to stay on the right side of this equation throughout life is an essential part of the human journey. In *Solitude*, Robert Kull's account of his time spent in Chile, he explains how he learned to let loneliness blow through him like a storm, watching it pass, knowing that it would.

THE BENEFITS OF BEING ALONE IN NATURE

To become grounded, we need to reclaim the art of being alone or, perhaps for the first time, develop the capacity to be by ourselves in order to reap its benefits. Indeed, a practice of solitude is more about the art of knowing and tolerating ourselves, as it is about being without others. How much solitude is useful is always a personal choice – the more you practise it, the better you will become at discerning how much is useful, and how much is too much. This is not a manifesto for becoming recluse.

Developing the capacity to be alone

A fear of loneliness can all too often turn into a deeply felt need to please others in order to be liked, in the hope of reducing the likelihood of abandonment. This prevents us from being seen as we truly are. It creates a gap between our true selves and how we present ourselves to others and can leave us lonelier than ever, no longer sure of our identity: we are back at the point we were trying to escape.

Tolerating what comes up for us in solitude is about moving into the safety within ourselves. It takes time to develop this inner trust – to know that we have our own backs and can advocate for ourselves, as well as keep ourselves emotionally, psychologically and physically safe. Conversely, developing our capacity to be alone is an important means of creating this requisite self-trust. This well-spring of trust is then available to us in all areas of our life. It can keep us grounded when interaction with others feel risky or unsafe. It can reassure us when we doubt ourselves or the world at large. It can help us enter more fully into relationships because we are secure in the one we have with ourselves. When we have a better appreciation of who we are and what we are capable of, the ground beneath us becomes a little more solid, and other people are a source of joy rather than fear or anxiety. We can be with them without needing more than they can give, and they can be with us without us giving more than we have.

Gaining time for reflection

Taking time alone in nature gives us the gift of space to think and reflect on the things that matter to us or are troubling us. It is a place to work things out, and a pause in proceedings. Many of us will be familiar with the instinct that compels us, during a heated debate to just go for a walk by ourselves.

Time alone provides a space to grieve for the things, relationships or people we have lost, or to prepare ourselves for a loss that may come. There is a particular type of solace to be found alone among the quiet rhythms of nature that is difficult to replicate in the amplified, discordant soundscape of the peopled world we inhabit most of the time. Being alone outside can create space for sadness to sit quietly

and rest in itself without the frantic, well-intentioned help of others to make it all better.

Solitude isn't always easy to endure during times of low mood and depression, and there is the danger of slipping into unhelpful rumination, but managed carefully and without fear, solitude can open a space for healing. It teaches us to just *be* with whatever *is* by ourselves, in the ambient fellowship of nature – to learn what is within us without being overwhelmed by it. There is no doubt that when we are alone, we are more likely to be confronted with a whole raft of feelings that seem to spontaneously bubble from the depths. Experiencing the feelings is healthy: learning to tolerate and regulate them is useful.

To tolerate what bubbles up in solitude is to sit with whatever comes. Learning to sit with uncertainty and difficult things, is to be with the feelings without needing to correct or change them, or rushing to resolve them. This is a vital life skill. Most people can connect with a difficult period of their life – a time that was hard but they coped and found a way through. Regulating what comes up in solitude is to reassure ourselves

> **When we have a better appreciation of who we are and what we are capable of, the ground beneath us becomes a little more solid.**

that we can deal with difficult things; that we can feel difficult feelings and also take measures to feel safe, comfortable and calm.

Developing self-reliance and self-belief

Solitude is a chance to listen more carefully to ourselves and to the natural world around us. It is an opportunity to shake off everything that *isn't us* – in other words, the things that get accreted to us over time, such as other people's beliefs, opinions and expectations – in order to come back to ourselves. Time alone with our own thoughts and beliefs allows us to make plans, reflect, ponder, grieve, celebrate and build personal capacity. It is a chance to be with ourselves and listen to our intuition; a chance to connect with creativity.

Solitude – outer, or inner – invites the question 'Who am I?' because if I am to be alone, then I had better know *me*: I better take this chance to get to know myself. In time alone, we are necessarily revealed to ourselves. We can no longer hide behind the presence of others but are forced to see and validate ourselves, where we might usually rely on others to do so.

Seeing what's there isn't always easy. Solitude quickly reveals our fears and anxieties, not least the ones we hold about our own inadequacies. We may become aware of how boring we feel we are, how intolerable our thoughts are, how paranoid we are capable of being, how fearful of our own shadow we have become. We might discover that we are not as capable as we thought we were, that we have been hiding a few things

from ourselves or that we have fault lines we didn't even realize were within us. A life lived only in company means we start living in the eyes of others. When we take others away, we have to establish how to live in our own eyes.

In many ways, we find solitude is a cure for loneliness. Solitude is a balm for the wounds it reveals. As is often the case in the plant world, as Robin Wall Kimmerer explains in *Braiding Sweetgrass*, the cure is often close to the cause. If we discover weakness in time alone by ourselves, being alone can also help us grow new capacity to face what's there. Thankfully, most of the fears we carry are overdeveloped and never come to pass. Time alone outside is a tried and tested method for building self-reliance and confidence in our abilities. Even in group activities, time alone is encouraged to consolidate learning, and offers a necessary counterpoint to the work that we can only complete with others.

When I have spent time alone on adventures, one of the most obvious fears is that I will not be able to look after myself; that I am too useless to be of any practical use to the frightened animal within; that I will wither at the first sign of a challenge. When I opt to

Time spent alone creates an environment in which we can hear the call of our wilder, intuitive selves.

continue the adventure and there is no choice but to carry on alone, then at the most basic level I find myself capable. This is an immediate rebuttal to the cry that *I am no good at this and I can't keep myself safe*. When, day after day, I am still safe, still fed, still watered, then I am faced with the uncomfortable truth that I am more capable than I think, and experience asks me to change my belief. If I hold on to the idea that I am incapable, I am being wilfully disingenuous: this is a great betrayal.

Developing our intuition

As well as developing self-reliance and challenging the unhelpful beliefs we might hold about ourselves and our abilities, quiet solitude is a chance to listen out for the small voice of intuition that sits within us. For some, listening to their intuition is a desirable but difficult practice. Perhaps they can't hear their intuition over the noise of competing demands, or they are more versed at overriding what they hear. Perhaps they have lost trust in what their intuition dictates if it has 'lead them wrong' before.

In our busy, peopled lives, it can be easy to forget how we want to live and that we have some choice in what

happens. Time spent alone creates an environment in which we can hear the call of our wilder, intuitive selves – the part of us that seeks to be self-willed and to do its own thing, and to flourish in the way we want.

Our intuitive voice is easily lost in a crowd, but solitude provides the chance to ask ourselves questions and to listen for the subtle signs of answers as they arise. I am not sure that anyone can describe definitively what intuition looks and feels like, but my understanding is that intuition is the voice within that is accompanied by a feeling or sensation of 'rightness'. That is, when I ask myself a question and various answers come to mind, I listen for the one that has a sense of 'Yes, that's the right one'. I can feel this in my body, most often in my stomach. It might have a tingling sensation. It might come with a deep sigh. It might even come with an upswell of fear.

Right is not the same as easy, and solitude has no interest in revealing what is easy. People often ask me: 'How do I know the difference between the fear that accompanies an intuitively right answer, and fear that arises because something might be dangerous for me?' I usually answer that the fear that comes with intuition still has a sense of *rightness* about it. The fear that comes from genuine danger is just cold, hard and wrong.

Creating better relationships

Connection is a vital part of how we flourish. It is our intrinsic need to stay connected to our own species that encourages us to invest in relationships, trying to make them the best that they can be. For many, this requires time alone to refresh and reset. Solitude is not a rejection of others, but a welcoming of the self which enables us to return rested and rejuvenated and better able to be with others.

This is not just because the world can be difficult, but because we can be difficult too. We are all prone to fraying around the edges when we are stressed. I can become unpleasantly offish when I'm tired; I get angry and shouty with too much exposure to the twenty-four-hour news cycle. Time alone in nature

is not just a chance to save myself from others but a chance to save others from me. I value the people who I share relationships with and want to give them the best of me, just as much as they want to receive it.

For most people, time alone will always be bookended by returning to contact with others – whether that's going home to a partner, meeting up with friends or simply returning to places where people are present. As unity moves to chaos, silence to noise, so solitude moves to company.

It is my experience that when I return to others after a period of solitude (whether after a longer trip, or just a few hours) I take less for granted, and arrive back wholehearted and authentic, in better command of myself, my own boundaries and my various needs and desires.

PRACTISING SOLITUDE IN NATURE

To practise solitude, we must first accept that lonely feelings will come and go. To endure loneliness is to let it blow through us like a storm that will pass. When we accept the occasional storm, we can begin to open ourselves to the possibility of communing with ourselves.

When we first find ourselves alone, we may find ourselves in the grip of identity crisis: who am I when no one else is here? What do I like? Believe? Think? Feel? But gradually, with time, insight becomes possible. We can begin to discern who we really are in terms of our values, our needs, our wants. Opening up to ourselves can be painful, and sometimes we need some extra help to manage this process. When we face profound disconnection from ourselves, and from nature, it can often feel overwhelming and sorrowful. If this happens, it is wise to seek help from someone who can support you in dealing with what comes up.

When an occasion for solitude arrives unannounced, we can take it as a bonus opportunity to learn something new about ourselves, or to recognize that it might be beneficial, because in reality we could do with having some quiet time. Instead of regretting suddenly being alone, why not ask yourself the question: *'What can I gain from being alone now that I wouldn't have gained in company?'*

While solitude might find us, it is also something to be sought. When we seek it and consent to it, we begin to make a new relationship with being alone: it is something we want, rather than something we must endure. In the right dose, it becomes valuable and not a surplus. It becomes something to cherish. But if you are not used to spending time alone in nature, then solitude requires a plan. Planning for it means setting an intention and setting boundaries around the time, at least in the beginning, to create safety for yourself.

Once you have a plan, you can reassure yourself that all the bases are covered and fully enjoy the solitude. Developing a practice of solitude is about recognizing what challenges you and working with those limits. There is no obligation to go further than you want to, or to throw yourself beyond what is comfortable. For some people, fifteen minutes spent in intentional solitude will feel like an achievement, others will experience their most fruitful solitude

MAKE A PLAN FOR SOLITUDE

A simple plan could consider the following:

1. How long do I have available to make my own?
2. How long would I like to spend alone on this occasion?
3. Where shall I go that feels good and safe?
4. Do I want to do anything in particular while I'm out?
5. What time will I return?
6. Do I want to be by myself without strangers around, or would I feel better in the presence of others?
7. What shall I take with me that will be nourishing or supportive?

For longer, wilder trips you might also want to consider:

8. Do I have the right equipment to stay warm, fed, watered and physically safe?
9. Do I need to tell anyone where I'm going?
10. Do I know who to contact if I need help?

over a period of hours, days or even longer. There is no right or wrong way to be alone.

Reflect on how you feel afterwards
The parameters of solitude look different for everyone. Over time you will get to know how much you want, how much is too much, and how you want to spend your time. As you spend time alone outdoors, you will find the places that speak to you. Some places might seem especially fruitful, others not. Some might feel too isolated; others too populated.

Finding a place that feels good for you, where you can enjoy time by yourself and enjoy the nature around you, is resourcing yourself. It is providing yourself with a place where you can come home to yourself and the natural world. It will allow you to develop your own safe place of nature connection. It may look like a cave, or it may look like an open plain.

You might like to reflect on why you feel connected to this place. What qualities does it possess? What feelings does it invoke? How do you feel in yourself when you are there? Become aware of what it is like *to be you* in that place. Be curious about the type of landscapes that affect you, and why.

It is important to take the time to notice what nature can offer you as guidance. When we allow our connection with nature to flourish, the whole world becomes a mirror. Consider asking, '*What do I need to see?*', '*What am I ready to hear?*'

The beauty of time spent alone

Practising solitude is about establishing what level of being alone is beneficial and fruitful for us. To do that usually

Learning how to embrace solitude and making space to appreciate its quiet, reflective qualities can be a source of great personal strength.

involves a bit of a *rub*: that is, tolerating the discomfort that might arise but knowing it is within our control to step out and re-join others when we need to.

Some days, solitude may feel rich and fruitful, generous and open. Other days, it might feel fearful, vulnerable or exposing. Some days, solitude may allow us to empty all the negative thoughts and emotions we have been carrying around for so long. Other days, we may find that we withhold from ourselves, reluctant to let go of anything. How we interact with ourselves when we're alone is not always dissimilar to how we might act with others.

Learning how to embrace solitude and making space to appreciate its quiet, reflective qualities can be a source of great personal strength. The paradoxical beauty of time spent alone in nature is that eventually we may have a sense of ourselves dissolving. Having faced the trial of being alone, and met ourselves on the way, what becomes possible is a peace that brings us back to the whole world. In these moments, we forget the fullness of ourselves and perhaps all we hear is the sound of the whole world breathing.

WILD

HEADING INTO THE WILD

I am always on the lookout for signs of wildness. In nature, in myself, in others. For me, they signify the presence of something essential and alive, if not scary and unpredictable at times. Wildness manifests differently in everyone, resists definition, but has a richness, density and vibrancy that is immediately recognizable.

Wild is the part of us that takes us outside to climb mountains, catch waves and sleep in the cold under the stars. Wildness brings us into communion with trees and animals, the wind, the rain, and keeps us there even when domestication raises its eyebrow. Glimmers of wild might be revealed when we do things that we didn't think we could do, or when we behave in ways that we don't expect of ourselves. They look like declarations of independence, intentions to be subversive, and resolutions to be different. Sometimes they are things that we label as impulsive or spontaneous. They sneak in but also burst out. They are angry, perhaps scary, in their own ways; they might feel both familiar and unfamiliar. They might carry a threat of some sort, perhaps to sanity or the status quo. Wild, is the small voice that talks back. It is the big questions we ask and the untidy, messy part of us. It is our unpredictability: the bit that resists boundaries, restrictions, and the word *should*. It is our changeability, boldness and tenacity. Wildness is the part of us that dreams. It is the uninhabited ideas. It is our longing. Above all, wildness is freedom. I like working with this human wildness; I like working with human wildness in wild places.

Nature has something to tell us about how to be wild.

HOW DOES WILDNESS GROUND US?

Defining *wild* is complex. It resists containment and labelling. Any attempt to capture it, package it and name it only diminishes it. Wild is something we are ambivalent about. We both fear and revere the wild, wrestling to tame it at the same time as fighting to preserve it. Wildness is at once unknowable, but also in our DNA. We have come from it, fleeing indoors to avoid it, but have never really left it, or even wanted to. Our relationship with wildness is as confused and paradoxical as wildness itself.

Nevertheless, nature has something to tell us about how to be wild. That is, how to live more authentically and less artificially. Wild nature also prepares us for some of the harder realities of life, such as how to live with fear, balance risk and stay safe. By meeting wildness outside, and embracing the same wildness inside, we can be more in-tune with nature and become more grounded in ourselves.

Helping to rebalance modern life

Our modern lives have become more indoor-orientated, more algorithm-lead and increasingly designed around being efficient and productive. From the moment we wake up to the time we go to bed, our busy lives are full of routines, responsibilities and regulations that keep things ticking over and keep us on the straight and narrow. Some of these structures we design for ourselves to keep a life full of dreams and ambitions on track and measurable, but others have become the norm through no direct choice of our own, such as the nine-to-five working day punctuated by set mealtimes and breaks. When we look in detail at our lives, it is easy to spot the many ways in which our paths have become somewhat predictable. While this helps us to get things done and can bring a great deal of comfort, there is no doubt that we also need and enjoy diversity, change, and a manageable amount of unpredictability and risk. Connecting with the wildness in nature is a chance to remember something of our own history, when we used to live more instinctively on the land and move with the seasons, and were less confined to the artificial strictures that have kept us in routines that don't track nature's rhythms. Staying in touch with the forces and energy of wild nature helps us to balance routine with uncertainty and for this unpredictability to become familiar and natural again.

> **Connecting with the wildness in nature is a chance to remember something of our own history.**

Becoming 'self-willed' and letting go of control

Wildness can be understood as something that is self-willed – self-initiated, self-governing, self-determining. We could also call this *freedom*. Nature shows us how to do this sort of wild, and this way of being wild

exists everywhere. Self-willed is daisies growing in pavement cracks. Self-willed is wildlife thriving in demilitarized zones. Self-willed is bird nests in the eaves, deer on derelict wasteland and rivers defying our engineering. It is plants at high altitude, desert lizards, urban foxes. It is you living your life your way.

To be interested in wildness is to be interested in relinquishing control – whether that's the tight control we hold over ourselves, or the control that we have over the rest of nature. To embrace wildness is to give up some degree of control and let a different force do its work. Self-willed is letting wildness return and, maybe sometimes, take over. Intuition is the driver of human wildness. To find our wildness and become grounded we need to let instinct help us to make decisions, rather than relying on reason or external advice alone.

We can find wildness if we set our own course and self-organize around the way we want to do things – it is saying 'Yes' because we trust in what's right for us. Wildness is borderless; it goes where it goes, where it needs to. It doesn't say,

'That place is not for me'; instead, it flows into the overlooked spaces, through cracks and into wherever it might thrive. Wild is uncultivated and is simply what it *is* and what it needs to be. Wild resists tight control and heavy management: it is autonomous and agentic, tenacious. Wild is authentic.

Becoming authentically you

When we live in a manner at odds with our nature, we become captive – we experience what it is to be suppressed and inauthentic. Existentialists might describe this as living in *bad faith*. We become a cultivated thing for others but work against ourselves. We can get caught in a holding pattern of anxiety and despair, feeling that the life we want is passing us by, or that the person we are can never be seen. Living in this sort of tension keeps us stressed, worried and eager to please everyone at the expense of our own wellbeing. We become well-meaning but often miserable, depressed, or despairing, living in a state of compromise between who we want to be and who we think we need to be.

> **To be interested in wildness is to be interested in relinquishing control.**

While compromise is an essential requirement of relationships, self-expression and freedom is also a requisite of fulfilment and wellbeing. We are at our most gracious and giving best for others when we are living in the uniqueness of ourselves. Being who we are, what our wild nature asks of us, is essential to becoming solid, centred and grounded. The path may not be an easy one, but it is nevertheless ours to take.

Improving your relationship with fear

Fear of the wild is as natural as our love of it. With biophilia comes biophobia, and ever since the human species evolved, natural fear has kept us alive. To connect with nature through fear is as instinctive as connecting through love. It is easy to let a persistent late eighteenth-century Romanticism obscure the real *nature* of nature. To imagine that nature is only green and pleasant, soft-edged and there for our comfort and solace, is to ignore catastrophic natural hazards, poisonous plants, dangerous animals, wildlife-borne diseases and the myriad other challenges presented by harsh natural environments. While nature offers us unprecedented opportunities to heal, thrive and connect, the deep and unknowable wildness of nature has no regard for our comings and goings. Natural forces can decimate whole communities in a moment, and many people across the planet live under constant threat from nature's inhospitality, explosive volatility and indiscriminate power.

Wildness, by definition, is the unknown and unpredictable, which means that we can't ever be completely sure of an outcome. Wildness is not linked to a set behaviour we can depend upon; it is not a benevolent force designed to work in our favour. The fearful wild is to be taken seriously and our challenge is not to eradicate it, but to live better alongside it. To respect it; to give it space. The same might be true of the wildness inside ourselves.

Stepping into wild places when we are prepared, we often realize that our worst fears are unfounded.

Managing our fears

Encountering wildness outside in nature, or within ourselves, is not always easy, but by doing so we can learn how to manage our natural fear response. The wildness of nature invites us to respect its power and take precautions. The risks we take need to be weighed in probabilities, which we must work out according to our own

BE YOURSELF

To help you on your journey to authenticity, start noticing from today *one thing in nature* that is simply being itself, doing what it needs to do, and living fearlessly *as it is*.

tolerances. Stepping into wild places when we are prepared, we often realize that our worst fears are unfounded, and those that remain can be managed and endured. We can live with some degree of fear when we know that we are equipped to face it. By facing fear in small, manageable doses, we expand our window of tolerance and find capability and strength within ourselves. Wildness teaches us how to coexist with our fears of the unknown. If we don't ever face the wild outside or within, we cannot entirely know what we have in us to deal with it. Dealing with fear of the unpredictable, unknown and risky wildness that life presents is essential if we are to keep our feet safely on the ground.

Accepting our wildness

Wildness is often suppressed or ignored. We, like nature, are wild on a spectrum: wildness lives within us to greater or lesser degrees, largely forgotten but often emerging, or trying to. Most of us exist somewhere between happily domesticated and feral-by-aspiration. In many ways, we are less wild than ever. Most of the world's population lives in urban areas. We are hyper-connected as never before. We are more sedentary and office-based than any previous generation. However, the fact that we are still an exploratory species, that we find enduring exhilaration in expanding our knowledge and comfort zones and seek wildness *out there,* is testament to our ongoing desire to reach the wild, and perhaps bring it closer to home within ourselves.

In seeking wildness in the rest of nature, we are, perhaps, looking for a mirror – reassurance that our wildness is okay and fits into the grander scheme of things. We might also be looking to hook our own wildness into a place where it belongs. Taking our wildness back into the landscape is a way of merging and interconnecting. There are few instances that are as unifying and life-affirming as the sense of our (human) selves dissolving into the rest of nature; this is when we meet nature's elemental power with the feeling that 'This is where I am supposed to be'. This is true *presence* within the rest of the living world.

WHEN IT'S TOO HARD TO SEE THE WILD

There are wild places within us that can feel hard to acknowledge or analyze. We don't always know what's there, and we are afraid to look for fear of being overwhelmed or consumed. Sometimes we know what's there but can't face it. We throw things into the wild place to try and satisfy it without having to look it in the eye. Food, alcohol, drugs, unhealthy relationships, and many more things beside. Quite quickly the wild places within us can become a type of oblivion and a place of annihilation. Sometimes these places become so fearful that we dissociate from them altogether. Getting even the gentlest feel of what that wild place might be, and seeking professional support to work with it more healthily, might be one of the most compassionate acts of self-care we can offer ourselves.

COMMIT TO THREE WILD THINGS

Spend some time exploring what being self-willed means
to you. Consider the following:

- What sort of things would you be doing if it was entirely
  up to you?
- What things do you dream of but don't feel able to do?
- Do you know what your intuition is telling you right now?

Commit to doing three wild, self-willed, things that will set
you on track to becoming more confident and grounded in
yourself.

Start with doing something smaller this week, then something
a little bigger in the next three months, culminating in
something really wild in the next year. Choose things that will
stretch you, but also build your confidence. And whatever
you do, don't ask someone else to give you the answers.

SEEK WILDNESS EVERYWHERE

To stay in touch with everything that is alive and vital, we first need to notice it. Wildness is made available to us all the time. It is not a place in the world that we cannot afford to travel to. It is not wilderness.

By imagining that wildness and wilderness are the same, we have come to believe that the only way to experience wildness is in true wilderness, and that anything else is neither wild not valuable. We have come to prize wilderness as the highest expression of 'true' nature at the expense of 'everyday nature' in our cities, backyards and edgelands. What is wild has become associated with *where people are not*. The risk of this thinking is that we forget the wildness everywhere, including in ourselves. When we forget the everyday wild in ourselves and our backyards, we set up a dualism that says the everyday is not worth loving and protecting, that wilderness is all that matters, that only places without human interference need our preservation. On the contrary, it is the wildness eeking out an existence within a few miles of our homes that needs our attention and our help.

In reality, very few places are untouched by humans. Wilderness is a place that may not exist anywhere as

much as in our own minds. But wildness remains: it lives everywhere, including in us. Connecting with our wildness is to connect with feelings of being alive and our innate biophilic tendencies. We need to look around our homes; roam a mile perimeter from our front doors; turn things over; look into corners and up to the sky; go where other people aren't going and learn to look beyond.

THE WILD CARD

In his book *Nature Cure*, the writer and broadcaster Richard Mabey talks movingly, of the 'wild card' that arrived in his life one summer. That is, the disruptive moment when nature deals us an unexpected hand which often marks an abrupt stop or turn-of-events requiring some sort of re-routing, and reconsideration of life as it was. The wild card might be unexpected illness, a bereavement, sudden loss, a disaster, attack or accident. It might also be an unsought promotion, love at first sight, an unexpected pregnancy, a lucky break or lottery win. It is a free holiday here, a ruined plan there. The wild card is a stopping force – something you did not see coming, something you could not have known would arrive. The wild card is what an inherently contingent universe

LOOK BEYOND THE OBVIOUS

The wild isn't something that only exists outside. It also exists in the 'middle space' of things we make, remember and imagine. It is something we recollect and bring to life in our stories, our poems, our music, our artwork, our photographs.

Spend some time connecting with the wild that exists in interesting and overlooked places:

- You could start with seeking wildness in the book you are reading or visit an art gallery.
- You can listen for wildness in your favourite songs, or in the photos you take.

When you start noticing wildness, you will see it in unexpected places: how it lives among us; how it's there for your discovery.

TAKE A WILD WALK

Most of us walk to places because we are trying to get somewhere. We might notice what's happening around us, or be completely blind to it. We are not so accustomed to walking aimlessly, and if we are, perhaps we are busy in thought, trying to solve a problem or make a decision.

Consider taking a walk with the express purpose of following the wild. That is, without a destination in mind, or even a route. Instead, be led by what shows itself to you as you walk. Follow the things that look and feel wild to you. If you see a bird, follow it. If you spot some greenery among the buildings, follow it. Let wild nature guide you and pay attention to what's there. Spend time with the wild, however small or inconsequential it feels to you at first. Know that wild *is* wild.

sometimes offers us, and we are simply left in its wake trying to work out how best to proceed, sometimes picking over the rubble, sometimes frozen to the spot.

While the vagaries of life can cut both ways, the lesson is the same either way. We must tolerate, endure and bear uncertainty about what is around the corner. We must find a way to live fruitfully and well, despite the risky act of being alive in the world.

Tolerating uncertainty is a recurring theme in therapy. Clients often come to counselling reeling from the effects of a devastating wild card, or anxious about the inherent uncertainty of living in a world where a wild card could strike at any time. Learning to bear what we don't – and can't – know, in order to carry on with life is the central work for an anxious mind. In honouring the wild card, we are nurturing a healthy relationship with ambiguity. We may need to lean into the things we don't know and remain ambivalent when surety is demanded of us by others who have forgotten the wild card. We can continue to count our blessings and live in the moment, leaving certainty to the unwise.

Wild chance, inherent in nature, asks us to remember with humility our place in the order of things and in relation to others. Life is unequal, because we have made it so, but the wild card can give and take away. Everything can be turned upside down and none of us are spared in the end. Can this make us gentler and kinder to all? Can we work to bridge the great unequal divides that we have made within our own species and between others?

Honouring the wild card is more about raising questions than getting answers. This is the nature of wild uncertainty – it provokes more than it resolves. A great gift we can give ourselves is sometimes to say: 'I don't know, but I will keep asking and keep going. I will relax my struggle with uncertainty'. Indeed, the only reasonable response to the wild card is to live anyway despite the risks – to be prepared for change, but not to become anxious about what *is* or *isn't*; to live wildly, bravely and tenaciously in the present. Because there is nothing else to be done.

LIVE ADVENTUROUSLY

To live adventurously is to adopt a mindset that is open to challenge, risk, uncertainty and ambiguity. It is about

being bold in our decisions with the intention of living fully, courageously and wholeheartedly. It has nothing to do with physique, wealth, social status, demographics or upbringing. We can live adventurously whatever our bank balance or body shape. Living adventurously is actively pursuing the life we wish to live, rather than sitting back and waiting for it to happen to us. It is being prepared to mess-up, make mistakes, suffer setbacks and carry on anyway.

Living adventurously might look like geographical exploration but it might also look like changing job, starting a family, moving somewhere new. It might be choosing to work less, taking on a project we hanker for, making an important decision, and in many other unique and personal ways, taking a leap into the unknown.

By living adventurously, we open ourselves to experiences of fear and uncertainty, and how to overcome them. Through adventurous living we discover our own capabilities, our ability to cope and grow our capacity for resilience in the face of difficult things, like the wild card when it comes. There is no time like the present to consider what living adventurously might look like.

To live adventurously is to adopt a mindset that is open to challenge, risk, uncertainty and ambiguity.

The benefits of adventure
While living adventurously isn't about going on adventures, for many, adventure travel is an exciting way to experience nature while testing their capabilities in an unknown and challenging environment. Research has shown that adventure is great for personal development and for our overall sense of wellbeing and mental health: adventure builds resilience and can be hugely empowering if we overcome adversity and gain achievements. It may also restore our attention, reduce stress levels, and be useful in alleviating depression and anxiety, as well as supporting post-traumatic growth. Adventure has the power to change the narratives we hold about ourselves, creates opportunities for self-compassion and cultivates a spirit of self-forgiveness when we find ourselves doing better than we thought we could.

Adventure isn't about 'battling' or 'conquering' nature, but is often about overcoming our fears, exploring our potential and experiencing beautiful things that we wouldn't have seen if we hadn't left our comfort zone. Adventure may be a meditation, or a form of personal expression, or simply a way of connecting with other people. Adventure is for everyone, and there is an adventure out there to meet every need.

CREATE AN ADVENTURE

Designing my own adventures is something I do regularly, as it enables me to tailor something that I will enjoy, be challenged by and grow through. What suits me won't necessarily suit you. Plan an adventure of your own so that you can feel the benefits for yourself. Below are a series of questions to help you build your own adventure:

- What kind of physical activity do you enjoy the most?
- Where in the world are you drawn to?
- What type of natural environment feels interesting, exciting, safe?
- Where can you get to that's affordable and accessible with the resources you have?
- What sort of thing motivates you as a reward? For example, going a long distance? Doing something on your own?
- Do you want to see other people along the way?
- Do you want to carry your home with you, or stay at places along the way?
- What do you want to get out of this adventure?
- What do you want to learn about yourself or your world?

MYSTERY

THE VALUE OF MYSTERY

In previous chapters, we have remained firmly rooted to the ground but considering the mystery of life is an invitation to zoom out to a universal level. In truth, it is hard not to. Many of the things we find most mysterious as humans are big issues with indistinct edges that remain unknown.

Science has helped to answer a lot of the *hows* and *whats* related to life on earth, but it hasn't explained the biggest *why* – why are we here at all? Why do we die? Why do bad things happen to good people? Why is there suffering?

To talk about mystery is to contemplate the mysterious nature of all things; it is to disappear down rabbit holes and worm holes. Struggling with life's mysteries and unanswered questions can easily leave us ungrounded. While exploring the big questions and unknowns of life is an entirely normal part of the human condition, and can be hugely fulfilling, it can also lead us into spirals of frustration and despair, as well as anxiety and depression. This is especially true when we ruminate on difficult issues that don't have an answer or a reason and get fixated on trying to solve the unsolvable.

Nature cannot answer our *whys* or explain its own existence, but coming back down to earth and connecting with the nature that is in front of us can ground us in the present; it can help us live more peacefully with uncertainty, and show us that a mysterious life can be a beautiful and exciting life.

GOING OUT INTO UNKNOWABLE NATURE

Taking ourselves outside and surrounding ourselves with nature, it quickly becomes apparent that there are many things we don't know, understand or have explanations for. As soon as we meet another pair of eyes, we are immediately met with *unknowing*. I can take an educated guess at what you are thinking if I meet you, but I cannot tell you what a bird is thinking. We might be able to name things with varying degrees of accuracy, or recognize sounds, or be able to say a little bit about what's going on with weather and plants, planets and atoms, but there is a lot that we don't know at the micro and macro levels. We still don't know much about why there is life on earth at all, or why some species adapt and survive when others don't. We know a lot about natural hazards, but accurate prediction still evades us. There's still much we don't know about bacteria, viruses and disease.

The troubling fact of mystery is ever-present in nature and therapy. The things we don't know tend to act as a *full stop* to the pondering that we sometimes do together. In many ways, mystery has the last word. I don't know why bad things happen to good people; we don't know why loved ones leave us too soon, or even when love will arrive in our lives; why we feel lonely, lost or depressed for no obvious reason; sometimes we don't even know why we got so lucky. Many things can be traced back to a beginning, but an equal number of things evade deduction.

It is the mystery, confusion and anxiety of loss that brings many people into therapy, and it is the same loss that takes many people outside during such difficult times. Outside, we see that nature is inherently messy, imperfect, uncontrollable and unknowable. While this represents a significant challenge for us practically and psychologically, because it goes against our socially and culturally instilled expectations that life will unfold with some degree of ease, practicality, control, linearity and knowability, it can also be reassuring.

The mystery everywhere in nature reminds us that it is normal and inevitable that there will be many things we don't understand.

The mystery everywhere in nature reminds us that it is normal and inevitable that there will be many things we don't understand. Bearing with uncertainty and living a life anyway is a universal experience when you are part of nature. When we go outside filled with confusion and anxiety about what we don't know, we are surrounded by everything else that is living in its own anxious process: there can be solace in shared experience.

NATURE IS IMPERMANENT

The fact that so much is uncertain in life is reflected in the impermanence of nature: everything comes and goes. We are confronted with nature's seasonality and cyclicity every moment of our lives – through birth and death, the turning of the seasons, the phases of the moon and the ebb and flow of tides.

Almost everything has a moment of ending, and a moment of beginning again. At times, this impermanence can feel calming, affirming, the only comfort that is left. At other times, it can be of no comfort and feel anxiety-provoking, depressing, lonely, or frustrating. This paradox is another mystery of the nature of things.

Nature offers us an intellectual frame of reference for endings and death, reminding us that both are inevitable. It also offers us proof that life continues and begins again. Making a deeper emotional connection with that which is impermanent is a time-honoured way of easing the pain of grief, loss, change and the uncertainty that life brings. Immersion in nature helps us to come to terms with *endings* and gives meaning to and connection with things that have been lost, it offers solace and can reveal something of what might come after. Everything grows, matures, decays and dies, but there is also rejuvenation, new growth and restoration. Things remain; there is matter and energy. In the impermanent cycle of life, there is a constancy that we can depend on.

There is also constancy in community and connectedness. We are not alone in things ending; we are not alone in grief; we are not the only ones who have to live without answers. As Biologist Andreas Weber comments in *The Biology of Wonder*: 'Perhaps one of the most important psychological roles that other beings play is to help us reconcile ourselves with pain, our inevitable separation as individuals from the remainder of the web of life, and our ephemeral existences'. For as long as life continues to regenerate itself, bringing new growth, there is hope. By taking ourselves outside and connecting emotionally with animals, plants and landscapes, it is possible to create a sense of meaningful togetherness with nature through our shared impermanence. This is a different type of relationship to the one we cultivate with humans, but it can offer us something timeless, transpersonal and grounding which transcends the brevity of human time.

Accepting that nature is inherently mysterious – that it is unknowable and impermanent – can tell us something about 'what to do' about mystery in our lives. It can help us to become a little more grounded and resilient despite the inevitable uncertainties and difficulties that come our way.

In the impermanent cycle of life, there is a constancy that we can depend on.

GROUNDING THROUGH RITUAL

In many secular parts of the world, we have lost the rituals and routines that previously helped us mark life's transitions and changes, and which grounded us in a natural cycle. As a result, we have lost processes for naming, honouring and grieving, and also ways to celebrate seasonality. While we may send flowers on the birth of a child or bring nature into our death rituals in the form of floral tributes, we have become less observant of other milestones that we experience along the way. As Robin Wall Kimmerer reminds us, in indigenous cultures, rituals are a way of bonding with nature. 'They focus our attention into intention.' Even the most homemade ceremony transforms the mundane to levels of sacredness that 'resonate beyond the human realm'. Consider creating nature-based rituals to mark losses, to honour endings, and to celebrate the continuation of life as well.

Whether you are struggling to accept the end of a relationship or are marking the end of one period of your life and the beginning of another, you might consider signifying the transition with your own nature-based ritual. You could:

- Take a walk of purpose, dedication or for a specific goal.
- Create a safe place in nature. This might be as simple as a place you return to over and over again; where you feel at home. It might be a quieter corner in a wood or a bench in the local park. It's about making a psychological connection of safety through familiarity and routine.
- Undertake a pilgrimage to a natural site that's personally significant for you.
- Light a fire.
- Plant flowers or a tree.
- Make symbolic use of water, such as a water feature.

HOW CAN WE MAKE USE OF MYSTERY?

When we can connect with the brilliance of nature, when we are struck, as if for the first time, by how miraculous it is to be here at all, under a sky full of planets and stars, pulled on by the moon, then we are reminded of something bigger and more mysterious than ourselves that doesn't necessarily need or provide any answers. For a moment our worries, anxieties and fears are stopped in their tracks, and everything becomes still around the magnificence of the present moment, and the whole universe beyond our comprehension. If we allow it to, the grounding force of mystery can provide perspective, opportunities for contemplation and for awe.

Be present

Engaging with the big questions and trying to understand these mysteries of life is being somewhat either in the past or in the future, and almost always in our own heads. It can take us away from feeling calm and transport us to an internal place of worry and unhelpful levels of rumination. Going outside and observing nature – the 'here and now' – at any given moment, is to arrive back in the present. Simply being with

PEAK EXPERIENCES

For those who are open to experiencing mysterious nature, there is the possibility of finding moments of deep aliveness, wonder and *clarity*. In the 1960s, psychologist Abraham Maslow first described 'peak experiences' as moments of 'rare, exciting, oceanic, deeply moving, exhilarating, elevating experiences that generate an advanced form of perceiving reality, and are even mystic and magical in their effect upon the experimenter'. He recognized, along with many other subsequent researchers, the power of peak experiences to promote a joyful and fulfilled life, their ability to offer increased awareness and understanding, a sense of being 'at one with the world', and feelings of joy and elation. They are significant in their own right and can be 'spiritual' in their reach, offering a transcendent glimpse of the divine, numinous nature that exists beyond our knowing.

Peak experiences can't be manufactured or forced: they are elusive. Instead, we have to create opportunities for ourselves where they become more likely. As they have long been associated with interactions with nature, the best advice is to be adventurous outside. Push your own limits sometimes – go higher, deeper, further when you can, take some calculated risks, set a goal and achieve it – and most of all, be receptive to the possibility of peak experiences happening at all.

nature *as it is*, in all its unknowability and impermanence, is to sit with mystery without needing to solve. The past is a memory, the future is a wish, the present is the only time we have. Everything that we *have* in the present is exactly what we *need* to be in the present. We should take nothing for granted, let humility for what is in our lives right now flow into the worried places. Try not to stress about what is coming or not coming but recognize that everything has its time in nature: to everything there is a season. Be here now.

Everything that we *have* in the present is exactly what we *need* to be in the present.

Be open to wonder and awe

Awe is how the universe makes itself known to us: perhaps it is the fleeting glimpse behind the curtain; maybe it is a divine encounter. What meaning you take from moments of wonder and awe might largely depend on your underlying world view or spiritual beliefs, but it is clear that the experience of wonder is positive and, for a moment at least, connects us with a mystery that doesn't always need a *why*. These moments help us sit in mystery.

When you see a murmuration of birds, the likelihood is that you are struck first by its visual beauty and its noise, you do not need to know *why*

it's happening to enjoy it or to feel the goodness in the experience. Noticing beautiful and mysterious things, from the tiniest movements to the most jaw-dropping spectacles, has the power to connect us to life-affirming, grounding, somehow-magical and paradoxically transcendent feelings, which are a welcome counterpoint to the harder experiences and encounters of life.

A moment of wonder, in itself, is an enjoyable experience that has the potential to connect us to the sheer beauty of our living planet. However, exciting new research also tells us that feelings and sensations of awe may reduce inflammation on a physiological level, and also make us friendlier and kinder to each other.

While there may be fewer opportunities to tap into wonder and awe than to notice everyday nature, having a mindset that is open to the possibility – where you are 'looking to see' – increases the likelihood of these experiences occurring. The next time there is a clear sky at night, why not go and look for the stars. Some of the most beautiful things to be seen in the world are mysterious: a great number of things are beautiful *because* they are mysterious.

Stay curious and confused

Curiosity is the driver of creativity and openness; it's something we are all born with, yet sometimes forget or outsource to others. To stay curious, or become curious, is to orient ourselves towards mystery, because what lives in mystery is possibility. Mystery makes different outcomes possible, sometimes even likely: every possibility has an inner door to another outcome. It is an inconvenient but liberating truth that we thrive on mystery. While at times it leads to suffering, we also get a great deal of satisfaction from seeking answers and creative solution making. Indeed, to be alive is to be inside the continual unfurling of our own wild imagination.

Curiosity allows us to move with the changes that might otherwise bring us to our knees. If we let curiosity meet mystery, then we can slow down the panic response. We can ask: 'What is this?', 'What new things might come of where I am?' or 'What am I scared of?' These are good questions to ask our anxiety, and can open up a whole world of conversation with ourselves.

As the poet Rainer Maria Rilke advocated in *Letters to a Young Poet*, we need to 'live the questions' and also 'live everything' in spite of the questions that have no answers. If we get on with living, he suggests, we might find what we seek at the end of the day anyway. We need to be patient with what is unsolved within us, and even learn to love what is unresolved.

In therapy, I always encourage this approach. While counselling is, on the one hand, a route to knowing and greater awareness, it is also a way towards accepting and tolerating our unknowing. It is sometimes recognizing that awareness *is* understanding that we can't know it all.

Wisdom often reveals itself in the moment it needs to be known – not a moment before. With this in mind, we might usefully sit with our confusion more often and recognize the clarity that can come from accepting what we don't know. There is a great deal of peace that can be found in saying 'I feel no certainty about what's ahead, but I accept the mystery'.

Make meaning

Life, as with nature, is not a problem to be solved, and neither are you. As a problem-solving species we find this hard to accept, so the 'solution' we have come up with is to make meaning. If we can't

> **It is an inconvenient but liberating truth that we thrive on mystery.**

WHEN CONFUSION GETS TOO MUCH

Inside a building, whether it's full of other people or not, if my thoughts are tangled and messy then confined spaces can compound my frustration and leave me feeling irritable, imprisoned, despondent or even more confused. Going outside throws open the windows of my busy mind and allows a bit of fresh air and light to get in.

If you are feeling confused, simply walking in a straight line at a slow, meditative pace can be remarkably powerful. This basic act can introduce energy into the places where you feel stuck and calm your body: through your body you will be enacting the way you want your mind to be. It breaks rumination and (if you let it) can flood the mind-body system with new things to see and experience beyond confusion. Going out into perfectly, imperfect, messy nature can be a unifying experience.

know the facts, then we make meaning with what we have. Ascribing meaning is arguably a more productive or enriching project that *knowing* facts because it isn't reliant on the burden of proof. In seeking or making meaning, we are acknowledging the incomplete picture, but recognizing that we *have enough* to be getting on with.

Making meaning is a way of understanding and bringing order into our lives. In some ways, it is an appeal to reason but, unlike deflating mystery through scepticism

and reduction, it usually involves an opening out or expansion to the bigger picture, a universal point, or the creation of something newer and bigger. Finding meaning in the inexplicable, unspeakable or downright painful is a way of bringing calm back into our lives. It can facilitate acceptance and forgiveness, even in the absence of a happy ending. It can also connect us to others through shared experience and make us more resilient as individuals and communities.

Unlike facts, the personal meaning we attribute to events and experience can change over time, and there is no required end to the process. As we generate new meanings, we go on learning the lessons of our lives.

Making meaning is a way of understanding and bringing order into our lives.

How we generate (and communicate) meaning is a wide and varied pursuit, reflected in the ongoing decisions we make, the conversations we have, the stories we tell ourselves and each other, the creation of myths and allegories, the music we make, the words we write, and the pictures we draw.

This entire book is, at its heart, about making meaning through our connection with nature, and how to make further meaningful connections over time. Nature can offer us a great literal and figurative space to explore meaning. We can take our dilemmas outside, but also connect with nature to broaden our viewpoint and perspective. Nature enriches our life with context and gives us a lot to learn and use to make meaning. It invites us to live the questions.

Much of our unnecessary suffering is based on our fear of impermanence, and the deep desire for things to be different than they are. If we can be with what is – however anxious the mystery – and realize that uncertainty and confusion doesn't damage us in any substantive way, and if we can make meaning of what remains, then we have the chance to stand gently in the heart of mysterious nature knowing that for better or worse, everything belongs.

SOME QUESTIONS I LOVE

When you notice that you are drawn to certain things in nature – perhaps a specific place, a landscape, a type of weather, an animal, a favourite tree – ask yourself some of the following questions and see what comes up:

- Why am I drawn to this?
- Why does this matter to me?
- What does this do for me?
- How does this help?

PERSPECTIVE

CHANGING OUR PERSPECTIVE

Time in the mountains has taught me so much about myself, but also what it means to be a little person in a big world, to have trifling problems in the global context. In the mountains I have found solutions, discovered my fears and found my place. Everything has been made possible by the literal and figurative change in perspective that they represent.

Whether it's a big mountain or boutique peak, to be among landforms that have existed in geological time is to be made smaller. Mountains cut us down to size, make us humble, but also – miraculously – embolden us. Their vastness often calls us forth into the fullness of our best selves, inviting us to push beyond our personal limits, while simultaneously revealing our cosmic irrelevance. It is a heady combination that is hard to resist.

I have been climbing and journeying in the mountains my whole adult life. From the Andes to the Atlas and the Alps, from the Cairngorms to the Carpathians, the *highlands* of our planet have been drawing me in and helping me live a fulfilled life since the moment I realized I couldn't do without them. Many people have written beautifully on the allure and 'call' of the mountains, highlighting the many

personal and collective ways that these remote landscapes speak to us. What you get from the mountains will be deeply personal, but time and time again common threads emerge. Our highest, and sometimes most deadly, places offer us an unrivalled opportunity to get above the peopled world and change our *perspective*. Elevated far above tiny towns, people and animals going about their daily business, mountains and their summits offer us a chance to get distance from, and find clarity in, our short-lived lives below.

Therapy, as well as spending time in nature, also allows us to broaden our perspective on the lives we have lived and are living, to take a wider view, and to consider the ways in which we can look at things differently. In therapy, we can look at our worries and problems from different angles, consider alternative views and 'look in' on our situation from different hypothetical vantage points. I see the bringing together of both nature and therapy as a winning combination that has the power to facilitate meaningful changes in perspective that can help with our overall feelings of wellbeing, but in the absence of time with a therapist, time spent in nature can stimulate some of the same outcomes if we are open to it.

> Changing perspective often requires us to slow down, reflect and think beyond our usual defaults.

HOW CAN GETTING PERSPECTIVE IN NATURE GROUND US?

To be grounded is to have a steady head in a crisis; it is to behave with measure and calm in a difficult situation; it is to feel stable in a complicated and messy world that is full of day-to-day challenges. Being able to see things from a different angle, being able to empathize deeply with others, and being able to get a different perspective on what is happening to us in our lives, helps us to find the stability we need to survive and thrive. Changing perspective is a cognitive skill that is vital for human living, and it's something we naturally do very well when we have the time, space and humility to put it into practice.

Changing perspective often requires us to slow down, reflect and think beyond our usual defaults. We can do this anywhere, but getting outside in nature affords both a break from our usual environment and offers us a whole territory of things that are living their lives from a different viewpoint. Connecting with nature provides a much more embodied way to change perspective. When we can really see, feel and experience life through a different lens, we are much more likely to absorb the benefits of that changed perspective than if we just think about it in abstract. Truly experiencing a different way of seeing the world is more likely to influence our future thought patterns and behaviours in beneficial ways.

Different perspectives offer different solutions

Going outside into natural places and moving around generates a different way of thinking in most people. Simply changing our environment, and opening our mind to different stimuli, can inspire creative solution making. Outside, surrounded by other life, we are invited to see what it feels like to view the world differently. Slipping into the vantage point of a bird, or the timeless mind of a tree, moving through a tangle of woodland, or breathing in the sea air from a cliff, all offer different

perspectives from which to reflect on our own issues. Solutions might not be directly transferable between our life and that of a bird, but everything in nature can offer us a mirror through which to reflect on our own situations and consider alternative ways to think and feel. How we move our mind around complex problems, and how we move our bodies through different terrains, can prompt different ways of thinking, opening up new possibilities.

You are part of a bigger picture

Very few people appreciate having their suffering diminished through comparison with other people's misfortune and pain. All too often, the notion that 'worse things are happening elsewhere in the world' comes freighted in judgement. It rarely alleviates the person's suffering, instead creating shame and guilt when they are already having a hard time. Getting out into nature, letting ourselves be absorbed in the rest of the living world and feeling part of the bigger picture of life is not the same as dismissing our pain as irrelevant (although sometimes we might come

to this conclusion ourselves). On the contrary, building a connection with nature allows us to situate ourselves gently among everything else that is living. Watching waves pound the shore or wind batter the trees, seeing animals hunker down in a hard winter or plants struggle through droughts – all of these things and more remind us that we are not alone in having to deal with life's difficulties.

This recognition doesn't necessarily solve the problems we face, or change what we feel, but might in some small way offer solace in times of need and reduce the isolation of our suffering.

Recognizing that we are part of a broader ecology of life that is also seeking to survive, also reminds us that the problems we are experiencing do not exist in a vacuum of individualism. Looking beyond ourselves to the interconnected environment that we live in, we are better able to see that much of what pains us is not our fault, or exclusively the result of 'bad decision making' or 'lack of resilience'. We are surrounded by inequalities in the set-up of life at community level, national and international levels. Through no fault of their own, people often find themselves marginalized, silenced and unsupported. Zooming out to look at the global context of life with its myriad inequalities and unequal pressures, which are reflected in our own lives, we are invited to be gentle on ourselves.

Not everything is our fault. We cannot solve everything that hurts us by ourselves. In an interconnected world, much of our sickness is shared: when the land is sick, we are sick; when our communities and support structures are broken, we are likely to feel broken too. The rest of nature does not – as far as we know – spend time punishing itself for negative outcomes. Nature simply does its best to live. We too can learn that self-compassion and self-forgiveness are vital for staying grounded. Not everything has to be accepted as it is, but nature can help us understand that we need to find a way to accept *ourselves* and carry on as best we can, despite (and sometimes in spite of) the things we're struggling with and against.

Nature can help us understand that we need to find a way to accept *ourselves* and carry on as best we can.

Staying grounded in kindness

Considering the broader environment that we belong to is a vital component in developing a grounding connection with nature. For some – hopefully all – of us as we reconnect with our innate

WHAT WILL YOU DO TODAY FOR NATURE?

Consider how you find it easiest to express love and work with your love language. If words are your chosen form of expression, speak them; if acts of service show you care, do them.

If you do nothing else, start with speaking lovingly about nature so that we normalize a collective, permissible, everyday love of the wild that takes us beyond a narrative in which nature is just a resource or capital.

Name, specifically, what is beautiful and say it fearlessly.

Speaking with love encourages kindness and respect. No gesture is too small – every humble gesture or observance can grow into something bigger.

biophilia (love for all that is alive and vital in nature), we deepen our empathic connection with life beyond our own species. Just as time spent truly listening to another person develops our empathy and understanding, enabling us to imagine walking in their proverbial shoes for a while, putting aside our personal world view, tuning in to nature, and really noticing what is happening beyond our human position, develops our empathy for other living beings. Empathy is important because it is related to compassion, or kindness; and when we feel empathy and connectivity, we are more likely to behave kindly, compassionately, and with care for the world beyond ourselves.

This empathic connection with nature is good for us and for the planet, even if it doesn't always feel like it. In the current climate, to become attuned to nature is to recognize that man-made problems have caused nature to struggle. This can impact our wellbeing and mental health, but by engaging with the challenges ahead and living purposefully in connection with nature it is possible to increase our *eudaimonic* wellbeing – that is, wellbeing linked to reaching our potential and living a fulfilled, purposeful life, even if choices along the way lead to periods of distress and suffering. Connectedness with nature is a predictor of both eudaimonic and hedonistic wellbeing, as it offers moments of pleasure

and happiness in the here and now, as well as fulfilment over a longer period.

A mutually beneficial relationship

Connecting with nature invites us to shift perspective from a position that is primarily human or egocentric to a viewpoint that is more 'eco-centric'. To look at life and nature from an eco-centric position is to remove our own centrality and to see the many ways in which life is interconnected. It involves adopting a more nature-centred worldview in which we play a part but are not centre stage, top of the priority list, or entitled to claim a higher value. Eco-centrism dissolves the divide between *human* and *nature*, and places intrinsic value on all of life, not just our own. Connecting with nature is a means of becoming part of something bigger – loving something larger than ourselves.

Recent research undertaken at the University of Derby (UK) has revealed that nature connectedness is a reliable predictor of increased pro-environmental behaviours, giving weight to the claim that what we come to *know* we are more likely to value and what we value we are more like to care for.

Building a two-way connection

As we deepen our connection with nature, we may start to care more about what is happening to it locally, nationally or internationally. Likewise, as we tap into nature's wellbeing benefits, we may feel the urge to 'give something back'. A reciprocal connection with nature is vital for both of our futures. If we do not return our care in attention and action that nurtures and restores then we are stealing, not sharing. Reciprocity may look like a lot of things. Just one of them is a language of love made alive through connection.

How we express love and gratitude can be deeply personal. Some people will plant trees, others will sign petitions. Some will lobby governments, others will step up their recycling. Some people will stop flying, others will eat less meat. Some will make a home for nature on their balcony, others will conserve water or switch to green power. Some people will tell others about their love of nature on social media, others will share their nature-inspired creations with the world.

These are just a few examples of things that are popular at the moment, but how we show our love and care is valuable however it is manifest.

What will your nature story be?

In counselling, I work extensively with stories: the ones we tell about our lives, the ones we tell about others, the ones we tell ourselves about the world, and the multiple combinations thereof. Story-telling is how we construct our realities and bring order, sense and meaning to the lives we have lived and are living. Some of our stories are bad and have sad endings, some are heroic and testament to triumph over adversity. Our stories really matter.

Every living thing leaves a trace, whether it's a chemical signature in water, a fossil in the ground, or a footprint in the mud. As humans, our stories are our trace – proof that we have been here at all. We tell them in everything from cave paintings through to the art and music we make, the expertise we offer, the records we set, the family tales we tell. Stories reveal what we care for, what we love, what we believe is valuable. They capture something of importance worth preserving.

As such, our nature stories are both a way of describing what's important in the here and now, and a means of rewilding and reconnection. How we talk about nature, how we explain our role within it, what we celebrate and name as important to us, all these things and more are a way of getting back in touch with our innate love of nature. By keeping our biophilia alive in words and stories, we have the opportunity to leave a meaningful trace of our relationship with nature, and perhaps keep alive that which needs protecting. In a world where biodiversity and individual species are being lost at a frightening rate, and where we are increasingly aware of the existential threat to our planet – both of which we have caused through our unchecked encroachment into every space on earth – there is the risk that we become individually and collectively numbed to the problem and withdraw our attention altogether. This is ducking out of our responsibility to the rest of nature and to each other.

Our nature stories are both a way of describing what's important in the here and now, and a means of rewilding and reconnection.

Telling our nature stories, talking about what we love and find meaningful, healing and valuable is a way of bringing back feeling and sensation to the numb parts of our mind. It staves off indifference born of disconnection. When we are psychically cut off from reality, we have nothing to offer the planet and are unhealthy in ourselves, but if we tell our stories, gently or stridently, we can begin to ensure that what matters is remembered before it's too late. The more we name what is being lost, the greater the chance that our collective numbing will be reduced: we need the collective to act. Stories that are acted on keep hope alive for the rest of nature, and for us. It is hard to be grounded without hope: it saves lives.

CREATE EXPERIENCES AND MAKE MEMORIES

No story can be written without events and experiences that make up the plot. For a story to emerge, things must happen. We must feel something. To tell your nature story, you must go out and experience nature:

- Notice nature, explore it and connect with it.
- Find the things you care for, the things that make you smile, the things that make you cry.
- Pick things up, get wet and muddy, let yourself become over-tired by a long day out.

These experiences are the foundations of your story and how you will speak of what matters to you.

Try writing a 'nature experience' wish list, set yourself a daily nature challenge, or commit to learning deeply about something in nature that catches your imagination.

GROUNDING IS COMING HOME

In the final analysis, becoming grounded might be equal parts of going *out* and *coming home*. To be grounded, is to put our feet on solid ground and put down roots or anchors within ourselves. It is to find safety in the container of ourselves and know that we are capable, adaptable and *here*.

Becoming grounded is a way of belonging to our minds and bodies. But being grounded is more than simply belonging to ourselves – it is also coming home to nature, of which we are a part, physically, psychically, emotionally and spiritually. It is coming home to the ground under our feet and finding a place to belong among everything else that is alive. Nature is a place of belonging for each of us and for every other species on the planet. We belong with each other as much as we belong to ourselves, and this relationship begins when we step up and into the connectedness we have explored in all of the previous chapters.

If you are feeling disconnected from nature, and ungrounded in your own life, now is the time to let nature help you find a way home.

FINAL THOUGHTS

Regardless of whether the mental wellbeing benefits of connecting with nature can be proven through science, or whether the power of connection is rooted in the meaning we ascribe it, becoming more grounded in our relationship with nature is good for us both physically and mentally, and can be hugely beneficial to the planet. It is not science but love that will bring us back to nature time and time again. Love that we feel instinctively in our bones at an ancestral level, love for what is being lost, love for ourselves and each other and the great wish to alleviate suffering, love for the wonder and precarious brilliance of being alive in the universe on a beautiful planet. The love that is biophilia. Maybe we will never truly understand why nature works, but when have we ever truly understood love and connection? These processes have always been somewhat mysterious and will no doubt remain that way.

There are gross inequalities in access to nature, but I hope this book offers a blueprint for what's possible and that you have found something useful, personal and resonant in these pages. Perhaps from there we can all work together to spread the word and lobby for equitable access in our communities and beyond.

While time spent in nature will not always be a *cure* for what ails us, a connection with nature can be *transformative*. This relationship has the power to transform how we see ourselves in the world and may transform a great many things beyond our immediate mind-body wellbeing.

It is often repeated that the climate crisis is a crisis of *mind*. That it is within our grasp to make the personal changes we are capable of, and lobby governments to make the systemic changes that only they can leverage as our elected spokespeople, but that it is a failure to *see the way things are* on the required timescales, that prevents progress. Our own health and wellbeing may also, at times, be a crisis of mind as well: a failure to see bigger, wider and more deeply. Nurturing a reciprocal relationship with nature has the potential to work deeply at the intersection of many of the world's most pressing crises as well as our own personal wellness, and send us off on tangible and spiritual adventures that will last us a lifetime.

> **While time spent in nature will not always be a *cure* for what ails us, a connection with nature can be *transformative*.**

SELECTED BIBLIOGRAPHY

Arvay, Clemens G. and Goodrich, Graham. *The Healing Code of Nature: Discovering the New Science of Eco-Psychosomatics.* Sounds True Inc, 2019.

Batchelor, Stephen. *The Art of Solitude.* Yale University Press, 2020.

Bekoff, Marc. *Rewilding Our Hearts: Building Pathways of Compassion and Coexistence.* New World Library, 2014.

Berry, Wendell. *The Peace of Wild Things: And Other Poems.* Penguin, 2018.

Caldwell, Christine. *Bodyfulness: Somatic Practices for Presence, Empowerment and Waking Up in This Life.* Shambhala Publications Inc, 2018.

Chödrön, Pema. *When Things Fall Apart: Heart Advice for Difficult Times.* Element Books, 2007.

Figueres, Christina. *The Future We Choose: Surviving the Climate Crisis.* Manilla Press, 2020.

Iyer, Pico. *The Art of Stillness: Adventures in Going Nowhere.* Simon & Schuster, 2014.

Jung, C. G. *The Earth Has a Soul: C.G.Jung's Writings on Nature, Technology and Modern Life.* North Atlantic Books, 2002.

Kahn, Peter H. and Hasbach, Patricia H., *Ecopsychology: Science, Totems, and the Technological Species.* MIT Press, 2012.

Kaplan, Rachel and Kaplan, Stephen. *The Experience of Nature: A Psychological Perspective.* Cambridge University Press, 1989.

Kimmerer, Robin Wall. *Braiding Sweetgrass: Indigenous Wisdom, Scientific Knowledge and the Teachings of Plants.* Penguin 2020.

Kull, Robert. *Solitude: Seeking Wisdom in Extremes - A Year Alone in the Patagonia Wilderness.* New World Library, 2009.

Mabey, Richard. *Nature Cure.* Vintage, 2008.

Tift, Bruce. *Already Free: Buddhism Meets Psychotherapy on the Path of Liberation.* Sounds True Inc, 2015.

Weber, Andreas. *The Biology of Wonder: Aliveness, Feeling, and the Metamorphosis of Science.* New Society Publishers, 2016.

Other publications:

Richardson, Miles, PhD. University of Derby, England. Various publicly available research publications and blog including: https://journals.plos.org/plosone/article?id=10.1371/journal.pone.0177186

Taylor, Richard. Research on fractals: www.theatlantic.com/science/archive/2017/01/why-fractals-are-so-soothing/514520/

University of Essex. Various publicly available research publications by researchers, including: https://repository.essex.ac.uk/27076/1/ijerph-17-01526-v2.pdf

INDEX

AUTHOR ACKNOWLEDGEMENTS

My warmest thanks are offered to everyone who has helped this book into creation, including Maddy and Jane at GMC, Sim for his photographic input and Lisa for getting it over the finish line. I want to offer my particular, heartfelt thanks to Victoria who started a fateful conversation with me in Gower Peninsula in 2019 at the same running festival, and who generously wanted the book exactly as I imagined it. I couldn't have asked for a better editor.

Thank you to Hayley who supervises my therapy practice so generously and rigorously, to the NR group members who have taught me so much, and to everyone I work with in therapy who puts their trust in me, whether we work outside or in. I care so deeply for you all.

Thank you to my dearest family and friends who have endured the various weathers of my mood as the book has progressed during an unprecedented time for us all. Especially Neil who has kept me well supplied with reassurance, tea and love even though I wouldn't let you read a word until it was done. You are my best person.

Lastly thank you to the rocks, to the trees in my village, to the earth. We don't deserve you, but you haven't yet entirely thrown us out. To every animal that has spoken with my heart since I was little. You have been my guides. This book is for the cat in the canoe.

PICTURE CREDITS

Courtesy © Ruth Allen: 16, 18, 24, 47, 50, 71, 74, 79, 91, 99, 102, 104–5, 109, 112–3, 118–9, 121, 127, 128, 145, 146, 149, 150–1, 154–5, 161, 165, 167, 177b, 181, 182, 187
Courtesy © Sim Warren: 4, 8–9, 12–3, 14–5, 22–3, 39, 48–9, 54–5, 56–7, 58–9, 68–9, 72–3, 80–1, 84, 92–3, 117, 124, 137, 139, 142–3, 177t, 178
See more of Sim's photography at:
www.theboulderprints.com and
www.instagram.com/simwarren

Shutterstock: 21 David Lade; 29 Hecos; 31 Allison Jehlicka; 32–3 Alex Yuzhakov; 34 David Pereiras; 35 Sasin Paraksa; 36–7 Olga Gavrilova; 42–3 EvgenySHCH; 53 Inga Linder; 64–5 Art Wittingen; 66 Ludovic Caritey; 67 Prapaporn Somkate; 77 wolff; 82–3 Juhku; 86 Kichigin; 89 Dean Pennala; 95 Skeronov; 96–7 Philip Reeve; 101 hofhauser; 103 Shen Stone; 107 Mikhailava Alesia; 114 Tony Campbell; 122–3 lavitrei; 130–1 andreiuc88; 134–5 siambizkit; 141 Matt Gibson; 157 Wirestock; 158–9 Menno Schaefer; 162–3 Tom Tom; 168–9 RudiErnst; 170 alenfra; 172–3 Damsea; 184–5 abriendomundo
Unsplash: 6–7 Torbjorn sandbakk 397baqfwzpi; 30 Kelly Sikkema; 44 Sharissa Johnson; 174 Dominik Resek